MANAGING COMPUTER RISK

THE WILEY/RONALD–NATIONAL ASSOCIATION OF ACCOUNTANTS PROFESSIONAL BOOK SERIES

Jack Fox • *Starting and Building Your Own Accounting Business*

Denis W. Day • *How to Cut Business Travel Costs*

Gerald M. Ward and Jonathan D. Harris • *Managing Computer Risk: A Guide for the Policymaker*

MANAGING COMPUTER RISK

A GUIDE FOR THE POLICYMAKER

GERALD M. WARD
JONATHAN D. HARRIS

A Ronald Press Publication
JOHN WILEY & SONS
New York • Chichester • Brisbane • Toronto • Singapore

Copyright © 1986 by John Wiley & Sons, Inc.

All rights reserved. Published simultaneously in Canada.

Reproduction or translation of any part of this work
beyond that permitted by Section 107 or 108 of the
1976 United States Copyright Act without the permission
of the copyright owner is unlawful. Requests for
permission or further information should be addressed to
the Permissions Department, John Wiley & Sons, Inc.

This publication is designed to provide accurate and
authoritative information in regard to the subject
matter covered. It is sold with the understanding that
the publisher is not engaged in rendering legal, accounting,
or other professional service. If legal advice or other
expert assistance is required, the services of a competent
professional person should be sought. *From a Declaration
of Principles jointly adopted by a Committee of the
American Bar Association and a Committee of Publishers.*

Library of Congress Cataloging-in-Publication Data:
Ward, Gerald M.
    Managing computer risk.

   (The Wiley/Ronald–National Association of Accountants
professional book series)
   "A Ronald Press publication."
   Includes index.
   1. Electronic data processing departments–Management.
2. Computers.   3. Risk management.   I. Harris,
Jonathan D.   II. Title.   III. Series.
HF5548.2.W318   1986   658'.05416   86-9115
ISBN 0-471-83233-2

Printed in the United States of America

10 9 8 7 6 5 4 3 2 1

PREFACE

Just when the computer age will arrive is no longer a question. It's here—spreading its tentacles into every facet of the business scene. Computer-assisted engineering and design, industrial robotics, electronic mail, distributed processing, automated-funds transfer, electronic-information retrieval, and decision-support systems are among the fruits of technology now heralding monumental changes in the conduct of business activities.

But the advantages of the computer age are not obtained without a price, including increased risk. Financial executives and other policymakers are concerned—and rightly so—about the business risks they face in this largely unfamiliar and ever-changing environment. Computer-related business risk increases with the number and complexity of systems and with an organization's dependence on computers. Computer risk also increases as centralized systems are dispersed via complex networks to a large number of points at far-flung locations. Selecting, installing, updating, and managing a computer-and-communications network can be a traumatic experience—requiring management to address a host of new questions.

This book is designed to help you, the policymaker, manage computer risks in the long-heralded computer age. It will help you assess whether those risks are minimized at a cost-effective level in your organization by careful and judicious planning and control.

The chapters that form Part One of this book deal with management-level strategic and implementation issues; these chapters are intended to give executives a perspective of the organizational areas requiring management attention. Part Two deals with the many technical concepts and products that need to be understood by the policymaker. Not all readers will need to read all chapters in Part Two in their entirety as the level of EDP-system complexity will vary widely from organization to organization.

The following are brief chapter summaries to enable you to find quickly what you need:

PART ONE—THE POLICYMAKER'S PERSPECTIVE

Chapter 1: Bridging the Gap

An overview of action for policymakers in managing computer risks; computer-related myths and misconceptions.

Chapter 2: Planning and Developing Computer Systems

Taking advantage of changing computer technology; planning with full consideration of potential technology changes; efficient and effective development of new systems.

Chapter 3: Minimizing Day-to-Day Computer-Operating Risks: Some Basics

Questions you should ask to determine if your organization has adequate controls surrounding day-to-day computer operations.

Chapter 4: Microcomputers: Changing the Risk Environment

The expanding use of the microcomputer in all information systems and the resultant changes in the risk profile of information systems.

Chapter 5: The Vital Link: An Effective Internal-Audit Group

The role of internal auditors in monitoring adherence to policies; the mutual objectives of internal auditors and data-processing management.

Chapter 6: Data Security: Ten Tough Questions

The ten most pertinent—and difficult—questions relating to data security in today's computer environment.

PART TWO—UNDERSTANDING THE TECHNOLOGY

Chapter 7: The Changing Landscape

The past, present, and probable future of computer technology, including a look at the use of distributed processing and database-management systems.

Chapter 8: What All These Computer People Do, and Why

Organization and management structure of a data-processing department; a review of typical job functions; changes that may affect organizational structure.

Chapter 9: Developing and Maintaining Systems

An example of a successful approach to design, testing, and implementation of new systems; approaches to program maintenance and changes.

Chapter 10: Hardware: More Than You Need to Know About Nuts and Bolts

Terminology and concepts useful in understanding contemporary computer hardware—from microcomputers to mainframes.

Chapter 11: Software and More Software

System and application software, including query languages, security software, and databases.

Chapter 12: Data Communications

Concepts and approaches to telecommunications and networks—from local-area networks to public networks.

All readers do not have the same degree of interest in every topic covered. Accordingly, "summary observations" are provided at the end of each chapter for those readers requiring only an overview.

GERALD M. WARD
JONATHAN D. HARRIS

New York, New York
September 1986

ACKNOWLEDGMENTS

Certain material in this book has appeared previously in publications of Price Waterhouse and is used with the permission of our partners. Acknowledgments are due many of our associates for their generous help. We also thank the National Association of Accountants for its sponsorship of the research study discussed in the appendix.

G. M. W.
J. D. H.

CONTENTS

PART ONE THE POLICYMAKER'S PERSPECTIVE

1 Bridging the Gap — 3
  Action required by policymakers — 3
  Myths and misconceptions — 5
  Summary observations — 8

2 Planning and Developing Computer Systems — 9
  Do you have a program to monitor emerging computer technology? — 10
  Is computer planning an integral part of overall business planning? — 11
  Does the organization of the EDP function promote effective working relationships and control? — 11
  Are EDP facilities managed with a view toward efficiency and effectiveness? — 12
  Before new systems or major modifications are authorized, are the associated computer risks addressed? — 13
  Are sound management approaches required for computer-development projects? — 14
  Are qualified individuals assigned to project teams to evaluate control issues? — 15

	Have policies and procedures been established for designing, coding, testing, and implementing computer programs?	15
	Summary observations	17
3	**Minimizing Day-to-Day Computer Operating Risks: Some Basics**	**19**
	Do you have adequate access controls?	20
	Who is responsible for the integrity of data and programs?	23
	Are duties properly segregated in all departments?	23
	Are processing controls adequate?	24
	What happens if processing is disrupted?	25
	Summary observations	27
4	**Microcomputers: Changing the Risk Environment**	**29**
	Increasing vulnerability	30
	Identifying risks	32
	Examples of the changing environment	34
	Policymaker action	39
	Summary observations	40
5	**The Vital Link: An Effective Internal-Audit Group**	**41**
	Investing in EDP-audit capabilities	42
	Responsibility for monitoring	43
	Auditor's objectives	44
	Data-security review	45
	Interdepartmental cooperation	46
	Summary observations	50
6	**Data Security: Ten Tough Questions**	**51**
	Ten questions	52
	Achieving a balance	56
	Summary observations	56

PART TWO UNDERSTANDING THE TECHNOLOGY

7 The Changing Landscape — 59
- The evolution of technology — 59
- Where are we headed? — 61
- Database-management systems — 61
- Distributed processing and smaller computers everywhere — 63
- The microcomputer explosion — 64
- Summary observations — 66

8 What All These Computer People Do, and Why — 67
- EDP steering committee — 67
- Organization and management — 68
- Changes that may affect the organizational structure — 70
- Systems and programming — 73
- Operations — 76
- Outside consultants — 79
- Summary observations — 81

9 Developing and Maintaining Systems — 83
- Systems development: How systems should be built — 83
- Software development by end-users — 91
- Controlling maintenance and program changes — 95
- Summary observations — 97

10 Hardware: More Than You Need to Know About Nuts and Bolts — 99
- Central-processing unit — 100
- Secondary storage — 102
- Data-input devices — 103
- Data-output devices — 105
- Summary observations — 106

11	**Software and More Software**	**107**
	Operating-systems software	108
	Language translators	110
	File-access manager systems	111
	Database-management systems	112
	Other systems software	116
	Application software	120
	Summary observations	121
12	**Data Communications**	**123**
	Communications hardware	124
	Transmission, circuits, and communications software	126
	Networks and service organizations	129
	Local-area networks	133
	Summary observations	138
Appendix:	**Microcomputer and Data-Security Survey and Results**	**139**
Glossary		**161**
Index		**181**

MANAGING
COMPUTER RISK

PART ONE

THE POLICYMAKER'S PERSPECTIVE

1

BRIDGING THE GAP

Financial executives and other policymakers traditionally keep a safe distance from computer-related issues, preferring to leave this admittedly complex area to computer professionals. But this attitude is changing, probably because computers are no longer limited to relatively routine processing activities, such as accounts payable and inventory. Computers are now integral to the overall operation of many businesses, including, for example, budgeting, strategic planning, and project-design functions.

ACTION REQUIRED BY POLICYMAKERS

Generally, today's policymakers recognize that they must take the lead if the computer risks that come packaged with computer benefits are to be understood and cost-effectively controlled within their organizations. Only policymakers have both the perspective to appreciate the consequences of computer-related problems and the authority to mandate actions necessary to minimize risks.

Managing computer risks depends fundamentally on management action in setting broad policies, goals, and standards; committing the necessary resources; assigning responsibilities for execution and supervision; and providing appropriate mechanisms to measure progress and performance. Such actions are as appropriate in coping with computer-related issues as they are in business areas that may be more familiar to the executive.

The adequacy of computer-related management policies and procedures must be individually determined for each organization. Centralized systems, distributed processing, database-management systems, and remote-terminal access all involve different levels of risk and need somewhat different kinds of controls. Also, some applications provide a pathway to valuable assets; others process information of little interest to anyone beyond a small group of users.

Controls provided to minimize risk should match the potential exposure. Further, there are many ways of achieving reasonable and well-balanced levels of control—from the relatively elaborate structures dictated by the size and intricacy of large systems to the heavy reliance on management supervision and user-department review of smaller systems.

Whatever the size and type of computer system, there are a number of policies, procedures, and programs that should be considered in most, if not all, circumstances; this book addresses those that are used by many organizations to minimize computer risk—both long-term and day-to-day risks.

Effective systems planning, systems development, resource management, and control over computer-processing activities are more important than ever. These efforts are essential in minimizing the long-term risks that affect all types of systems, including financial operations, management-information systems, manufacturing operations, office administration, or any other distinct operating segment. Failure to plan for your organization's future computer needs in today's rapidly shifting computer environment can be costly. An outmoded system, a system that does not match your operating pattern, an inflexible system, or one that simply does not contain effective computer-processing controls can lead to competitive disadvantages, missed business opportunities, and excessive operating costs.

Computer risks also are present in the day-to-day operations of all types of computer systems. These risks relate mainly to control. Appropriate control features, installed when the system is designed, and prescribed control procedures, in place during execution, help minimize risks of inaccurate or incomplete information, unauthorized access to data, use of the computer to misappropriate assets, and interruption of business operations. You will want to know that adequate policies exist for each of these. Before proceeding, let's consider several computer-related misconceptions.

MYTHS AND MISCONCEPTIONS

Have you ever heard the following statements?

> *"Our computer environment is very complicated—we have many different types of computer systems in different parts of the business. We can't set policies to cover such a wide range of computer systems."*

Don't confuse detailed procedures with management policies. Detailed procedures required to implement your policies must reflect the specific circumstances of computer systems and business environments. Minimizing the risks in a computer environment depends on attention to the assignment of responsibilities, development controls, procedures to ensure the integrity of processed data, and provisions for continuity of processing. In the absence of organization-wide policies, desirable control features are likely to be missing in many systems.

> *"We don't need to worry about computers; we rely on our DP manager and internal auditors. That's what we pay them for!"*

Obviously, it is appropriate to rely on the advice of professionals and specialists. But it is dangerous to let them make policy decisions that are management's responsibility. For example, engineers assess the technical aspects of product design and actuaries estimate pension costs. But engineers do not make final decisions on acceptable measures of quality control and actuaries do not establish benefit levels. The broad perspective of management is needed to set policy and establish goals, even in technically complex areas. You do not need to know the finer points of computer design to establish policies that minimize computer risk.

> "We paid top price for the best equipment. Certainly for that kind of money we bought good computer controls; our risk must be low."

Equipment reliability should not be confused with security or control. Although computer manufacturers generally have excellent quality control and maintenance programs, this alone does not produce adequate control over the processing environment. For example, data entered into a system must be authorized, complete, and accurate. Operating procedures must be established to prevent intentional or accidental misuse of the computer. Software must be designed, coded, tested, and implemented with adequate application controls in mind. These controls are not delivered with the equipment.

> "Our software systems were purchased as a package from a reliable vendor; these packages must have good controls."

Software controls are only as good as the control environment in which they operate; even the best designed systems may be ineffective if your people override or do not use the controls provided. You must determine whether your organization properly focuses on controls when acquiring software packages and whether your people use existing controls to minimize risk. Further, if the software you purchased was designed to serve the general purposes of many users, it may not employ the specific control features needed for your business.

> "Our data-processing applications must be responsive to our operating needs; controls over data processing slow down the system."

The question of data-processing control versus operating efficiency can only be answered after due consideration of all the issues. Management may very well be willing to accept a relatively high level of risk, but this should be based on sound cost-benefit studies. When that choice is made, it should be the result of a deliberate decision made at the policy level.

Obviously, computer controls should not become a bottleneck. Excessive controls or poorly designed controls may be inefficient, ineffective, or both. The time to address control questions is at the design stage. Usually, it is possible to introduce sound controls that reduce risk to an acceptable level without seriously affecting the timeliness or costs of information. Wrong decision resulting from quickly delivered but inaccurate information is only one of the possible consequences of inadequate controls.

"Computer technology changes so quickly that long-term planning is not worthwhile."

Planning now to take specific action at some time in the future is indeed fraught with uncertainty. But, you can be prepared to act when the time is right by making sure that computer developments are monitored in an organized fashion. It is likely that your people are already watching computer developments in their areas—manufacturing, research and development, information processing, for example—with keen interest. Consider assigning formal responsibility for keeping these developments under review and for reporting, at designated intervals, the status of technology that promises to meet identified organizational needs.

"The leading edge of technology can be sharp—we plan to let others lead the way."

There is nothing wrong with this approach unless it simply masks resistance to useful change. Learning about new technology and evaluating its possible effects on the organization's business carry no commitment to adopt that technology until it has been proven by others. As a matter of organizational philosophy, you may be eager to experiment with innovative technology in an attempt to obtain a competitive advantage, or, as a matter of policy, you may choose not to acquire unproven products. Neither approach is inherently right or wrong. Just be sure that your approach is the result of a conscious business decision based on a study of the facts, not just a matter of habit. Be cognizant of the fact that sound controls must be in place whether your technology is on the frontier or well proven.

SUMMARY OBSERVATIONS

Management must take the lead in ensuring that computer risks are understood and controlled by establishing broad policies and standards and providing mechanisms to monitor performance.

There are three principal areas in which you need to be sure you have effective EDP policies: planning and systems development, operations, and review.

The need for policies transcends the particular computer system; policies are required for all computer environments—from stand-alone microcomputer systems to sophisticated mainframe systems.

Although you often hear that controls slow down processing and are not needed by smaller organizations, these are myths that could cost both time and money. These comments are inappropriate considering the speed of today's processors versus those of the 1960s, when the cost-of-control myths were first established.

A program for monitoring emerging computer technology will help an organization to be in a position to take advantage of the best that technology has to offer in a controlled manner.

Neither adopting nor avoiding the leading edge of computer technology is inherently right or wrong; either approach should be the result of a conscious decision based on reasonable knowledge of viable alternatives.

2

PLANNING AND DEVELOPING COMPUTER SYSTEMS

Ideally, your computer system is an unobtrusive and efficient part of your operations, providing the information needed to solve business problems (often an essential part of the services rendered to customers) and helping to make good business decisions. But will it stay that way? Or will it become a business problem in its own right?

You can minimize problems by ensuring that your computer resources remain in harmony with your organization's needs. In the long term, a computer system poses a risk of becoming a bottleneck impeding your company's ability to compete in the marketplace and take timely action on business opportunities.

Advances in computer technology surely will continue. Developments from industry's laboratories offer business opportunities to streamline information processing, to effect cost savings, and to improve customer service. Unless your company has a program to track these developments with an eye toward identifying those suited to your needs, you may find that your competitors have gained an edge while you are continuing to cope with an increasingly out-of-date system.

Computer systems and the organization of the computer function should keep pace as operations expand, contract, or change direction. Unless information requirements are in your long-range plans, a currently satisfactory computer system could buckle under the load—

suddenly becoming too small, too slow, or improperly designed in the face of a changed operating environment.

If a new or modified approach to the use of computers is part of your future, policies are needed to ensure that the new systems live up to expectations.

DO YOU HAVE A PROGRAM TO MONITOR EMERGING COMPUTER TECHNOLOGY?

A structured program designed to identify and evaluate new technology and its potential benefits for your organization will help prepare for the future. Among the ingredients of a successful program are clearly defined objectives communicated to all concerned, specific assignments of responsibilities, provisions for reporting to management at designated intervals and, above all, full management support.

Information on changing computer technology is available from a variety of sources. For example, your computer professionals should be expected to:

Keep abreast of developments reported in trade journals

Attend industry seminars and trade shows to identify and evaluate available technology and future directions

Request from vendors periodic briefings and demonstrations of new products and expected future offerings of hardware and software

Perhaps your computer professionals should periodically develop and present to selected operating-unit managers update or background courses in current technology. The courses can be designed to promote audience participation and discussion of practical uses of the technology in your organization. Outside speakers and programs are also available.

A formal program for periodic policymaker review of computer-application opportunities helps pave the way for prompt action when the time is right for your organization to use this technology. It ensures that important new technologies are not overlooked.

IS COMPUTER PLANNING AN INTEGRAL PART OF OVERALL BUSINESS PLANNING?

Some industry observers predict that information-systems planning will be one of the most important business activities by the 1990s. Indeed, in some circumstances it is already.

Consider how data-processing plans fit into company-wide strategic plans. Are data-processing requirements considered routinely in formulating your organization's long-term goals or are computer-related activities planned in isolation? Even worse, are changes in computer systems customarily made on an ad hoc basis in response to operating needs that have already reached crisis proportions?

Given the substantial time typically required to implement new application systems, integrated planning is essential if your computer services are to keep pace with service needs. For example, some acquired application-software packages are difficult to modify in response to changing business needs. If your future business plans call for growth, then be sure your computer plans allow for growth! Be sure to integrate computer planning into your business planning.

DOES THE ORGANIZATION OF THE EDP FUNCTION PROMOTE EFFECTIVE WORKING RELATIONSHIPS AND CONTROL?

The segregation-of-duties principle—a cardinal rule in the days of manual accounting—still lives. Both the position of the data-processing function in your organizational structure and its internal organization are important if you are trying to achieve these objectives.

As alternatives to centralized computer-operating environments are adopted, lines of responsibility tend to become blurred and system design, program development, and computer-operations activities are more often performed at the local level. Maintaining adequate control in this climate requires careful attention to policies that ensure use of common standards. You might wish to consider the use of organization-wide methodologies. In general, control groups, such as data security, and system-design and maintenance groups, should have no responsibility for day-to-day operations.

The position of the EDP functions on the corporate chart should, in any event, promote an equal level of service to all user functions and a positive contribution by EDP management to the organization's goals. If, in accordance with a pattern that was logical several years ago, one of several user departments holds the EDP-reporting reins, that department is likely to receive preferential treatment—a source of dissatisfaction to other users.

Does the EDP department report through too many layers of management? Forced into such a situation, EDP management may become resigned to the status quo, failing to propose the action necessary to keep your computer services up-to-date. Although the exact position in the hierarchy will vary, the individual responsible for data processing should, at the very least, report at a level comparable to that of the managers of user departments.

ARE EDP FACILITIES MANAGED WITH A VIEW TOWARD EFFICIENCY AND EFFECTIVENESS?

The data-processing-operations department is fundamentally a production unit and, as such, improvements can often be made through the application of proven management techniques used routinely in other parts of your business. What type of internal departmental studies are underway to improve efficiency and effectiveness? Your computer professionals should have an up-to-date knowledge of matters such as:

Information requirements of user departments
Staff and skills required to meet user requirements
Effects of peak and normal workloads on computer and communications hardware and software requirements.
Performance and utilization standards for the equipment
Hardware and software best suited for long-term user requirements
Commercial availability of suitable application packages
Use of outside computer service bureaus and associated risks

As you would expect, computer applications should be responsive to user needs while minimizing operating costs. Your computer professionals should have a sufficient grasp of user requirements and an adequate, two-way channel of communications with users to ensure that:

Development and operating costs are well-controlled and do not exceed benefits

Each application system is producing accurate and reliable output that users consider timely and responsive to their needs

Charges (if allocated) for processing and storing data are fair and understandable to each user group and promote desirable use of these resources

If your organization does not seem to have appropriate two-way communications between user groups and computer professionals, perhaps it is time to reexamine assigned responsibilities and your organizational chart.

BEFORE NEW SYSTEMS OR MAJOR MODIFICATIONS ARE AUTHORIZED, ARE THE ASSOCIATED COMPUTER RISKS ADDRESSED?

Some organizations have systems with deficient controls simply because control issues were not addressed properly before the application software was acquired or developed. The time to define these requirements is before a new processing system or a major modification is authorized.

Ask some questions. For example: Given the level of personnel available and the organization's operating environment, is it likely that present control standards can be maintained? Is on-line update essential to meet the organization's information requirements or would slightly less current data serve equally well? If confidential data is to be placed in the system, how will it be protected from unauthorized access? Should it be placed in the system at all? Do cost estimates include provision for additional resources that may be needed for system administration and control? Is there a suitable software package that can be acquired as a cost-effective and timely alternative to internal development of new software?

As a matter of policy, project proposals detailing expected costs and benefits should include an analysis of potential exposures to computer-security risks and the proposed methods and associated costs of minimizing them. The information presented should be sufficiently extensive to permit senior management to evaluate the potential exposure, operating advantages, cost, and efficiency, and to make an informed decision as to whether the expected level of risk is acceptable. The acceptance of application software having less-than-desired control features because of cost or operating considerations should be a business decision based on careful evaluation of all relevant facts.

ARE SOUND MANAGEMENT APPROACHES REQUIRED FOR COMPUTER-DEVELOPMENT PROJECTS?

Computer projects require the same approach to project management as any other important project undertaken by your organization. New projects should not be authorized without a thorough cost-benefit analysis. After the decision has been made to proceed, project costs should be monitored continuously and the project reevaluated as each major phase is completed.

Many data-processing departments could improve their records for completing installations of new systems on time and within budget by using sound project-planning and control techniques. Policymaker enforcement of accepted procedures for cost estimating and project monitoring helps to ensure that project development is approved, scheduled, and tracked on an informed basis. At predetermined intervals, the policymaker should be furnished with clear, concise progress reports providing explanations of any significant obstacles encountered and stating the action planned to overcome them.

Be sure that user departments have fully considered commercially available software packages before authorizing the development of systems "from scratch." In today's environment, the cost of equipment and commercially available programs is declining; the quality and flexibility of packages are improving; and the cost of personnel is continuing to increase. Management should, therefore, seriously consider the practicality of purchasing software developed by others.

ARE QUALIFIED INDIVIDUALS ASSIGNED TO PROJECT TEAMS TO EVALUATE CONTROL ISSUES?

Control features are least expensive to incorporate into new or modified systems during the design stage. Systems should be reviewed at each step of development—design, programming, and testing—to ensure that adequate safeguards are built-in. Consider assigning responsibility for identifying these requirements to a project team member.

Systems designers and representatives of user groups may not have the appropriate training or may, unfortunately, view control measures as being of secondary importance. The need to provide controls may actually conflict with other goals. Accordingly, a project team, or even one individual, should be assigned the responsibility for evaluating potential risks and for determining that appropriate controls are provided before the system is implemented or even allowed to proceed beyond system design. This responsibility sometimes is assigned to the internal-audit department and sometimes to an independent quality-control group.

The designated individual or group should have the authority, subject to appropriate appeal procedures, to accept or reject a system feature or modification based on evaluation of the adequacy of control features provided. After design of these requirements, be sure that satisfaction is documented by project team sign-off after the system has been tested, but before it becomes operational.

HAVE POLICIES AND PROCEDURES BEEN ESTABLISHED FOR DESIGNING, CODING, TESTING, AND IMPLEMENTING COMPUTER PROGRAMS?

Computer programs should be designed, coded, tested, and implemented in an organized and controlled manner. Formal policies and procedures can help to ensure that this occurs. These policies should include provision for extensive user involvement in all phases of system development and implementation.

Both new and modified systems should be subjected to formal test and acceptance procedures by a quality-control group, internal auditors and, certainly, users. Test and acceptance procedures should ensure that controls specified during the design phase are actually included, that they operate effectively, and that only approved programs are used to process data.

Software programs are valuable assets that need to be protected. Program libraries that physically, as well as electronically, separate test versions of programs from production versions are a desirable means to provide this protection.

There will be occasions when there is intense pressure to get new or revised applications "up and running." Under those circumstances, the risk of disaster is perhaps greatest and specified test and acceptance procedures should be strictly enforced. Supervisory review, documentation of program changes, and tests by users and internal auditors should not be omitted for the sake of expediency.

Management should consider that changes in computer programs may very well affect the way other business activities are carried out. For example, changes to a finished-goods program may change procedures for obtaining sales orders and the timing of product shipments to customers. The effect of significant EDP changes on the business should be reviewed by management as well as user-department personnel.

SUMMARY OBSERVATIONS

If computer systems are not properly planned and developed, they pose potential risks from the standpoint of impeding your organization's ability to compete in the marketplace and take timely action in response to business opportunities. Computer planning should be an integral part of your overall business plans.

Your EDP function's place on the organizational ladder should promote the concept of an equal level of service to all users based on benefit and need and your organization's overall business goals. Sound internal organization of your EDP function is critical for control purposes.

Computer risks should be addressed as an integral part of the process of authorizing new computer systems or major modifications. At the same time, remember that computer applications are part of a larger system, with manual as well as computerized elements.

Computer-related projects require the same approach to project management as any other important project undertaken by your organization.

Internal auditors or quality-control groups should have responsibility for ensuring that major computer projects include sufficient control features.

Formal policies and procedures help to ensure that computer programs are developed and implemented in an organized and controlled manner.

3

MINIMIZING DAY-TO-DAY COMPUTER-OPERATING RISKS

Some Basics

Some of the risks discussed in this chapter are almost entirely products of the computer age. Others have been present in financial systems well before the introduction of computers. The speed and invisible recordkeeping characteristics of computer systems have made risks seem more insidious and have dictated different methods of minimizing them. An important point to recognize is that, despite often radically differing methods of providing control, the underlying control objectives in typical business applications do not change, regardless of the degree of automation. The general categories of day-to-day operating risks that must be identified and minimized are:

Unauthorized Access to Confidential Data Stored in the Computer System. Customer lists and product-sales data are examples of information that most companies would prefer to keep confidential. In addition, data stored in personnel and payroll files should be safeguarded to ensure employee privacy.

Unauthorized Manipulation of Data for the Benefit of Someone Inside or Outside the Organization. Examples of this are deliberate processing of improper sales entries to meet prescribed internal profit goals and obtaining (stealing!) assets by charging the organization for fictitious vendor services.

Inaccurate or Incomplete Information. Obviously, balances in the company's accounts will be misrepresented if inaccurate transactions are undetected and uncorrected and measures are not adopted to ensure that all transactions are properly recorded. If such steps are not taken, the accounts could be materially incorrect and management decisions might be based on erroneous data.

Interruption of Business Operations. Loss of financial or operating data or the loss of processing capabilities, whether accidentally or intentionally, can cause serious interruptions in normal business operations.

The degree of exposure to each category of risk varies enormously from organization to organization, within each organization, and among the various components of a single system. Some systems provide a pathway to valuable assets; others yield little opportunity for profit. Some information is highly confidential; other data in a system is of limited interest.

On-line access through remote terminals using dial-up communications presents exposures that are not present in the absence of this capability. On-line access that permits updating or changing information presents greater exposure than on-line access that permits only access to obtain or read information. Distributed processing, in contrast to a centralized system, has the potential for increasing some types of exposure while minimizing others. The characteristics of each individual system and subsystem must be considered in estimating the potential exposure of that system before determining the strength and type of control measures needed.

How do you identify and evaluate the computer risks you face every day? Where do you start? Assess your existing computer-related internal-control policies and procedures. The following are some questions you should address.

DO YOU HAVE ADEQUATE ACCESS CONTROLS?

In the days of the single-location computer facility, access controls meant protecting the equipment, programs, and data files from tampering through a system of locks, authorization badges, security

DO YOU HAVE ADEQUATE ACCESS CONTROLS?

checkpoints, and the like. No longer. Nowadays, the computer in that carefully guarded room is likely to be linked by telecommunications facilities to untold numbers of remote terminals. Stories of computer "hackers" who violate business-computer systems for "the challenge" are reported in the press more and more frequently.

Limiting access to the physical system components and programs—wherever they are located—is important in protecting the security and integrity of your data. But if the system can be accessed from remote terminals, including microcomputers, via communications facilities, a data-security system with programmed safeguards is a necessity. Such safeguards, coupled with appropriate policies and administrative procedures, help ensure that confidential data is not being extracted for unauthorized purposes, that assets are not being drained by data manipulation, and that your financial information and the programs vital to corporate operations have not been inadvertently or deliberately corrupted.

Programmed safeguards focus on access-control software that allows the computer itself to perform security checks on those trying to access computerized information. Typically, an appropriate identification code, password, and other information must be furnished by the potential user and processed by the access-control software program before access to any data is permitted. Data should be stored in the computer in such a way that a specific user obtains access only to specifically authorized data, while all other data is off-limits. Where the perceived level of risk so warrants, passwords may be encrypted (scrambled) to prevent disclosure during authorization checking. Consider the following when reviewing the use of identification codes and passwords:

> Authority and responsibility for issuing identification codes and passwords should be assigned. Rules for maintenance of this data (for example, a rule that users must change their passwords every 30 days) must also be clearly defined.
>
> Passwords should be changed periodically to guard against erosion of password confidentiality. A password assigned to an employee who leaves the company should be canceled immediately.
>
> A sense of the importance of maintaining strict password confidentiality should be instilled in your employees. Examples of a poor

sense of confidentiality: passwords written on a piece of paper and pasted to the top of a terminal; common words and employees' names or initials used as passwords; employees exchanging passwords for personal convenience.

An access-control system that permits nothing but read-only access should be used, where possible, to prevent data from being exposed to unnecessary risk. With read-only access, an authorized employee can obtain information but cannot change or add information to your system.

Automatic, computerized logs (created by system-software programs) should be used to record accesses to the system. Logs should be monitored regularly and repeatedly; unsuccessful attempts to access the computer within a brief time period (such as 10 minutes or so) should be investigated promptly.

Another important area of concern is the effect of the computer revolution on individual privacy. Computerized payroll and personnel records undoubtedly contain information about employees that many of them would consider confidential. Employee privacy is an emerging issue—part of a rising fear that personal data may be incorrectly or improperly extracted from a computer. Several countries have in effect, or are considering, various employee-privacy laws as well as laws that restrict transfer of certain data across national boundaries.

Carefully designed computer applications are capable of providing more access control and more privacy than manual-recordkeeping systems that rely primarily on the integrity of individuals. The potential intruder to a computer system needs access to data that can be stored in a form unreadable to the human eye, and access to such a system can be controlled by an effective set of data-security procedures and access control software.

The same access controls that protect other confidential information can promote employee privacy. Typically, a computer program checks that a request for data is legitimate by comparing certain user and terminal identifications with stored authorization tables. Records of unsuccessful attempts to use the system, as well as legitimate uses, are created automatically and are kept available for future examination.

WHO IS RESPONSIBLE FOR THE INTEGRITY OF DATA AND PROGRAMS?

Although protection of specific data files, programs, and related system and operation documentation is necessarily the responsibility of the data-processing department, user groups, such as the accounts-receivable and payroll departments, have proprietary interests (or ownership responsibility) in computer applications.

Users should be responsible for the accuracy and completeness of specific data files. Effective discharge of this responsibility demands that users also be responsible for the reliability of related programs. Users should have authority to request revisions to programs, to approve program and system changes before they become operational, and to obtain complete and accurate system descriptions from programmers and analysts.

In a database environment, responsibility for organizing data may be given to a third party—often called a database administrator. The database administrator usually is responsible for implementing user-defined rules for storing and accessing data so that conflicts among users are avoided. But specific users still "own" the data, as in traditional batch processing systems.

ARE DUTIES PROPERLY SEGREGATED IN ALL DEPARTMENTS?

Segregation of duties is a fundamental element of internal control. Data-processing personnel should record and process data, but they should not originate, approve, or authenticate transactions, perform final reconciliation of input and output, correct reconciliation differences, or have access to assets.

Segregation of duties within the data-processing function is essential in obtaining assurance that data is processed in accordance with approved procedures and that data is not subject to accidental or deliberate corruption during processing. Typically, this is accomplished by keeping responsibilities for day-to-day processing separated from responsibilities for system development and system changes. Operations, development, and program maintenance staff should be limited to read-only access to production programs, and then only as needed to perform their job functions.

Processing controls designed to preclude computer operators from processing erroneous entries can be bypassed easily by most programmers. Accordingly, programmers and analysts should not have access to programs and data files used for production runs. Changes in production programs should be made only in accordance with authorized test and acceptance procedures. Program testing should be accomplished using test files—certainly not the live files themselves.

Conventional segregation of duties may be difficult to maintain in a decentralized computer environment. For example, when small computers and terminals are placed in user departments in numerous locations, there may be too few employees at any one location to avoid an undesirable concentration of responsibilities for data origination and entry, computer processing, user authorization, and asset custody. Management should assess such situations carefully, recognizing the additional risk involved, and attempt to implement mitigating procedures (such as increased management supervision, reasonableness checks and independent sample/review of activity logs) tailored to the individual circumstances.

ARE PROCESSING CONTROLS ADEQUATE?

Processing controls are designed to maintain data integrity during the execution of computer programs. These controls aim to ensure that correct file versions are used, all data submitted is processed completely, inaccurate or incomplete data is captured and corrected and files are used only for authorized purposes. Processing controls include:

- Program-derived control totals matched by the system to user-department control totals
- File-balancing procedures to check the completeness and accuracy of master files and transaction files
- Automated operator console and job-accounting logs that record all program requests and operator actions
- Automated production-program libraries that restrict program availability for live processing to authorized personnel

Programmed edits to automatically check validity and reasonableness of input

Internal file labels written magnetically on the file medium to permit program verification of the file name and version number

Prescribed procedures should be in place to handle transactions rejected in the editing process because of erroneous data content, format errors, or failure to comply with other established criteria. For example, where data is processed in batches, rejected data should be held in suspense files until the users or a quality-control group can correct it. Since data located in suspense files may be the result of attempts to circumvent controls, clearance of items in a suspense file should be supervised closely. In a so-called on-line system, the adequacy of procedures for editing transactions submitted to the system is a key control requirement.

After processing is completed, output should be distributed to authorized users only. Users should be responsible for making sure that processing results are accurate and complete. They should verify that computer-produced results equal manually developed control totals or conform to reasonableness benchmarks and that all rejected transactions have been corrected and processed satisfactorily. Changes in critical master-file data, such as credit limits, names of approved suppliers, and employee names, should be reviewed with particular care. These procedures should be documented, understood by employees and enforced by management.

WHAT HAPPENS IF PROCESSING IS DISRUPTED?

The central role of computer systems in the operation of most organizations underscores the importance of measures to guard against and minimize effects of prolonged disruptions of computer operations.

Data-processing equipment, data files, programs, and system documentation should, of course, be protected from loss or physical destruction. Contingency plans should provide alternatives that will permit your operations to continue if data-processing services are interrupted by some unfortunate event.

Obviously, the cost of contingency measures should be weighed against the potential cost of the inability to function effectively until service can be restored. Different businesses have different exposures to failure of computer systems. At a minimum, consider the following procedures:

> Data files, programs, documentation, and backup and recovery plans should be duplicated and stored off-site according to a strict schedule.
>
> Written explanations of programs and operating procedures prepared in the course of program development and modification should be secured in a locked, fireproof location.
>
> Arrangements should be made either within the company, with another company, with the vendor, or elsewhere for alternative processing facilities in the event of a prolonged disruption.

Data-processing departments should develop written plans for recovery and restart of processing for use when a problem occurs. The plans should address the procedures for moving supplies and data under different types of emergencies, assign responsibility for specific tasks, describe formal and informal arrangements with vendors and others to supply compatible equipment and back-up facilities, and assign priorities to applications.

In addition to describing the mechanical aspects of restoring EDP and communication facilities, emergency plans should document procedures to be followed by user departments in the event of a failure. When the system is out of service for an extended period, the work ordinarily performed using the computer must be performed some other way. Alternative processing procedures should be established and tested beforehand, rather than in the hectic period following an emergency.

And, finally, do not forget to test the contingency plan on at least an annual basis. Better to get the "bugs" out of a contingency plan before it's the real thing!

SUMMARY OBSERVATIONS

Day-to-day computer operations are subject to several categories of risk: unauthorized access to data and programs; unauthorized manipulation of data and programs; inaccurate or incomplete information; and interruption of business operations.

Protection of computer data files, programs, and written program descriptions should be the responsibility of the EDP department. Accuracy and completeness of the data submitted for processing and the output should be the responsibility of user departments.

Programmatic-access control is essential whenever computers can be accessed from remote terminals. Data-security procedures help both to promote employee privacy and to protect corporate information.

Data-processing personnel should not originate, authenticate, reconcile, or correct transactions; these are responsibilities of the user departments.

Programmers and analysts should not have access to live programs and data as part of normal, everyday operations. Emergency access should be monitored carefully.

Plans to ensure continuity of processing when computer and communications facilities are out of service should address user-department procedures, as well as EDP-department procedures.

4

MICROCOMPUTERS
Changing the Risk Environment

Microcomputer proliferation in most organizations results in widely dispersed equipment and programming activity, scattered processing, and decentralized data and software storage. The control over the integrity of the information system (previously more centralized in the function) may tend to erode because information processing and storage and retrieval capabilities are increasingly in the hands of individuals outside the data-processing department. This change, however, should not reduce the need for solid controls and policies but, rather, should result in their redefinition and expansion. Adequate security and internal control for microcomputers require user involvement and commitment as well as leadership by management data-processing professionals.

Basic differences between mainframe and microcomputer environments must be appreciated in order to establish sound control systems. The personal nature of the microcomputer, for example, frequently enables one individual to perform the function of user, programmer, systems analyst, and operator. In the mainframe environment, however, segregation of these tasks is a primary and well-established tenet of internal control.

As discussed earlier, a well-run mainframe environment incorporates numerous controls over processing, including manual reconciliation, validation, and edit controls. In addition, the generation of an audit or management trail of critical activities is a standard mainframe operating feature. The typical microcomputer system, however, may be characterized by shortcuts in data approval, few processing controls, and a lack of activity reporting.

The operating environment of the microcomputer is generally more informal than that of the mainframe. Microcomputer applications can be written in an easy-to-use programming language or through use of the macro-programming capabilities of some of the more powerful off-the-shelf software packages. Although control over program changes, data security, system documentation, backup and recovery plans, and system design is firmly ingrained in most mainframe environments, microcomputer systems typically lack such protection.

INCREASING VULNERABILITY

The growing abundance of low-cost, easy-to-use microcomputers, together with increasing computer literacy, has transformed the once technical and recondite area of data processing into one that requires only minimal sophistication on the part of the user. As a result, computer misuse, at least in the form of information theft and misuse, certainly has risen greatly with the micro boom.

The increasing vulnerability of information systems is illustrated in the following figures. The baseline of each vulnerability triangle presented in these figures corresponds to the number of employees and outsiders possessing both the opportunity and approximate level of skill to commit computer-related improprieties. The elevation of each triangle represents the level of skill required to commit the improprieties listed to the triangle's right. These may be defined as:

Sabotage. Abuse, destruction, or theft of equipment

Data-entry fraud. Destruction, alteration, or disclosure of information entering the system

System Fraud. Unauthorized system use; destruction, alteration, or disclosure of application programs, systems programs, or data

Figure 1 depicts the vulnerability of the mainframe environment to improprieties committed by employees and outsiders. As illustrated, many individuals have both the opportunity and the relatively low

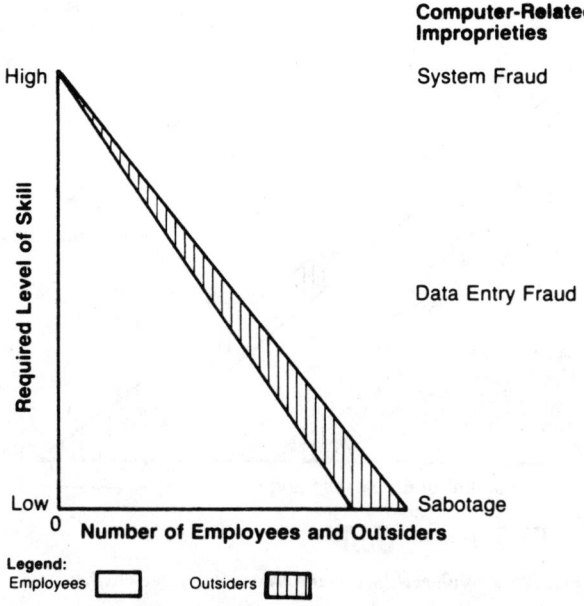

FIGURE 1. Vulnerability in the Traditional Environment

level of skill required to sabotage; fewer have the opportunity and skill required to commit input fraud; yet very few individuals have both the opportunity and the degree of technical ability required to compromise the operating system.

In Figure 2, the vulnerability triangle of the new microcomputer-pervasive environment is superimposed on that of the mainframe environment described. Again, the number of individuals with both the opportunity and the skill to commit improper acts diminishes as the activity becomes more complex. At all levels of the microcomputer-pervasive triangle, however, the number of employees and outsiders is larger than for the corresponding points on the mainframe triangle.

One reason for this increased vulnerability is that the dispersal of equipment in a microcomputer environment may not be restricted to the physical confines of the organization; many firms, for very valid reasons, actively promote the installation of microcomputers in their employees' homes. This distribution of computing resources increases the opportunity for abuse, destruction, or theft of equipment, software, and data by many more individuals. Instances of data-entry

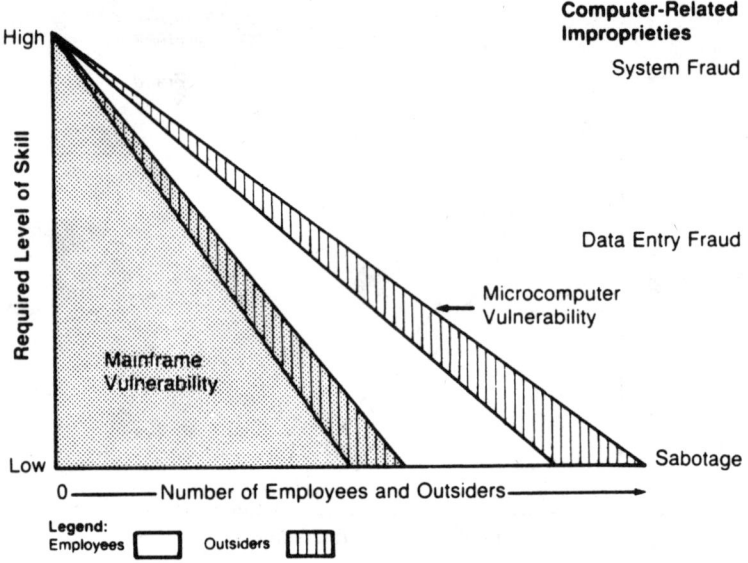

FIGURE 2. Vulnerability in the Micro-Pervasive Environment

fraud also become more common as more individuals provide input (especially when the microcomputer is used in distributed data capture processing). Finally, because a lower level of technical ability is needed to program or operate a microcomputer, more individuals have the requisite skills to compromise the system.

IDENTIFYING RISKS

To counter this increased vulnerability, organizations must approach security and control links in today's microcomputer-pervasive environment just as seriously as in the mainframe-only environment. The nature and uses of the microcomputer may, however, necessitate a somewhat less standardized approach than that used in a typical mainframe environment. The adequacy of the procedures followed generally depends on the microcomputer's use and the system's structure.

A three-step approach based on risk-assessment techniques is useful in determining the necessary controls. It involves identifying the exposures connected with the micocomputer application, assessing the degree of risk associated with the exposure, and selecting and implementing the appropriate controls in connection with cost/benefit evaluations.

Identifying Exposure

The potential effect on your organization of a detrimental event related to a microcomputer application should be assessed. Examples of detrimental events are fire, flood, power failure, machine failure, sabotage, and fraud. The effect on five key areas should be addressed when identifying exposure:

Operational Dependence. The effect on your organization's ability to continue regular activity if the application goes down.

Financial Implications. The extent of financial loss if a detrimental event occurs.

Information Sensitivity. The sensitivity of the data accessible to or processed by the system. How would your organization be harmed by the disclosure of data to unauthorized employees or outsiders?

Financial-Reporting Implications. The effect of a harmful event on the integrity of your organization's financial statements.

System Structure. The preceding areas relate to information either processed by or available to the microcomputer system. The structure of the microcomputer system involved also affects exposure. For example, a stand-alone microcomputer system with dedicated applications presents a risk profile different from that of microcomputers linked to a mainframe system available to many users. Thus, the impact of an undesirable event can vary dramatically with the system structure.

Determining Degree of Risk

The degree of risk associated with the exposure can range from low (virtually no risk) to high (extreme vulnerability). Potential adverse effect must be based on both quantifiable (money terms) and nonquantifiable (such as reputation) elements. Assigning a degree of risk to areas of exposure is useful when determining the required level of control.

Selecting Controls

The degree of risk associated with each microcomputer system determines the level of control desired and the individual controls to be implemented to attain that level. Controls that should exist to some degree in every microcomputer application can be categorized as follows:

> Backup and recovery procedures are needed to ensure that processing can continue and records can be re-created in the event of accident or disaster and that operations can continue in the event of employee absence or termination.
>
> Security procedures are needed to minimize the risk that sensitive or confidential information will be disclosed, data files or programs will be stolen or destroyed, and equipment will be used by unauthorized individuals.
>
> Software-integrity procedures are required to ensure that programs are performing the intended tasks and that the proper software is being used.
>
> Input/output controls must be designed to ensure that transactions are properly approved, proper files are being accessed or updated, all input is processed completely and accurately, and output appears reasonable and is properly distributed.

EXAMPLES OF THE CHANGING ENVIRONMENT

The following two situations illustrate microcomputer security and control problems resulting from differing system structures and applications and demonstrate the control-selection process.

Standalone Microcomputer Application

Let's say your credit manager uses a microcomputer to facilitate preparation of monthly reports to management. Assume the credit manager enters historical sales, receivables, collection, reserve, and write-off data into the microcomputer system. This information is obtained primarily from hard-copy reports generated by the central computing facility. Using microcomputer word processing and graphics software, the credit manager generates historical- and forecast-collection analyses, and a summary of the preceding month's activity. (These reports previously had been prepared manually.) The data diskettes are then stored off-line for use in preparing subsequent reports.

In this situation, the microcomputer is used as a standalone workstation with no communications access to the company's central computer. To determine the appropriate controls, one would begin by identifying the areas of exposure and the degree of associated risk, as discussed earlier. Here the microcomputer is being used primarily to improve the credit manager's productivity. In most similar situations, the occurrence of a detrimental event most likely would not jeopardize usual business activity, result in financial losses, compromise the organization through release of confidential information, or affect financial statements to any greater degree than if these tasks were performed manually.

Nevertheless, some controls should be considered even in this simple example. (Virtually every microcomputer application requires some of the basic controls.) In this case, the following controls would be applicable:

Backup and Recovery. All microcomputer users should be made aware of the need for backup procedures regardless of how the machine is used. Hitting the wrong key or spilling a soft drink on a diskette can destroy a month's worth of work. The credit manager should make copies of programs and historical data and store them in a safe place. Backups of data during lengthy data entry and/or processing should also be made frequently during preparation of monthly reports to avoid having to start from scratch if an accident occurs.

Documentation. Although perhaps not as critical in this situation as in one involving information processing, adequate documentation (usually, written instructions describing how the application works and what it is supposed to accomplish), and provision for the use of alternative equipment can be important. If the credit manager in this example were terminated or absent for an extended period, the work that he or she had performed could be useless without adequate documentation. Because the quality of documentation provided with commercial software packages varies, all such documentation should be carefully reviewed before a software package is purchased. Similar documentation-control procedures should be established for software developed internally.

Security of Data and Equipment. All diskettes or hard disks should be protected when not in use. Special attention should be given to those containing sensitive or confidential information. Although the hardware peripherals and software packages for small computers are relatively inexpensive compared with large computer wares, procedures should be implemented to minimize the potential for loss by theft or damage, whether accidental or deliberate. In this example, diskettes should be locked in desk drawers, and unauthorized access to the credit manager's office should be prevented.

Software Integrity. Each program should be thoroughly tested with sample data to ensure that the software is performing its intended tasks. Test results should be compared with the results produced by the current system (manual or automated), and problems should be identified and resolved before the program is used.

Input/Output. Proper labeling of diskettes, externally and internally, is essential to ensure that the appropriate file is being used. Manual procedures for detecting errors that occur during data input should be implemented. Matching input-control totals with output-control totals is useful. The controls used in this situation are simple and require little time or effort to implement. User training in security and control procedures is, however, essential because a very high level of user involvement is required to create a sound microcomputer-control environment.

Microcomputer/Mainframe Link

In this example, a workstation has a communications link to the mainframe. This more sophisticated microcomputer environment brings not only the potential of more benefit to the organization but also a higher level of exposure.

The credit manager has a microcomputer equipped with communications features providing online access to public databases maintained by outsiders. The microcomputer is also linked to the corporation's central computer.

In addition to using the microcomputer to prepare reports to management, the credit manager uses it to obtain financial information on new customers (through use of an outside database) and such information on established customers as available credit, sales, and payment history from the company's central files. The online connection is used for internal-review purposes as well as for responding to customer inquiries. The credit manager can also change a customer's credit limit on the central file by using the microcomputer/mainframe link.

In a typical organization, the following degrees of risk might be associated with this microcomputer application:

> **Operational Dependence.** No exposure, low degree of risk. The microcomputer's function is not central to continued regular business activity.
>
> **Financial Implications.** Some exposure exists along with perhaps a moderate degree of risk. Errors made when credit limits are input could have adverse effects. Credit could be extended inadvertently to undeserving customers or fraudulently to fictitious customers. Conversely, failure to increase limits to properly approved levels could result in poor customer relations and perhaps lost sales.
>
> **Information Sensitivity.** Exposure here could be high. Customer lists and sales-activity information could be useful to competitors.
>
> **Financial-Reporting Implications.** Although no direct general-ledger posting is connected with this application, some exposure exists in the financial-reporting area. As mentioned, errors or irregularities could occur when credit-limit data is input. This could

result in a misstatement in the balance of the reserve for a bad-debts account.

System Structure. Because the microcomputer has access to the corporation's central computer, exposure exists and the degree of risk is most likely high. The increased risk in the areas of financial implications and information sensitivity can be attributed to the change in system structure.

In addition to the controls prescribed in the first example, other controls should be considered. Because the major area of concern is related to system structure, controls should focus on this area. The following questions should be asked to define more clearly the risks and specific controls that might be appropriate:

What controls are in place to prevent unauthorized access to data and programs stored in the organization's central data files? Although it is appropriate for the credit manager to review customer accounts, is it appropriate for this individual to peruse the company's payroll or personnel files?

Is a record, or audit trail, created of unauthorized attempts to access or change customer data? Does anyone review this material?

Do controls preclude unauthorized changes to information within the central data files? In this application, the credit manager was authorized to change customer-credit lines. What other customer data can the credit manager change or delete?

Can changes made to data files be identified? Once credit limits have been changed, is there an audit trail indicating which accounts were affected, when, by whom, and by how much? If a record does exist, is anyone reviewing it?

Security must focus on both the organization's microcomputers and the mainframe. The credit manager's and others' use of the microcomputer in this example must be considered, as should the use of any other microcomputer equipped with communications capabilities from within or outside the company.

POLICYMAKER ACTION

The support and involvement of senior management and computer professionals are essential to the successful development and implementation of a sound microcomputer security-and-control program. In addition, these groups must recognize the many benefits of microcomputers as well as their serious control challenges.

Because microcomputers are mainly used by individuals outside what is typically considered the data-processing department, the insight and authority of senior management are required to ensure establishment of, and compliance with, an organization-wide microcomputer-implementation plan. Computer professionals are needed not only because of their acknowledged responsibility for maintaining the integrity of an organization's information system but also for their technical expertise.

The next step is the development and implementation of organization policies and procedures governing microcomputer acquisition and use. These guidelines should comply with overall corporate short- and long-term information-system goals and security and control requirements. They should, however, be flexible to foster creative as well as productive microcomputer use. After procedures have been implemented, they should be monitored regularly to access the adequacy and continued effectiveness of controls.

In addition to actively participating in the development of microcomputer guidelines, management should establish a support function to oversee organization-wide microcomputer activity. This function, which can be assigned to one or to a group of data-processing professionals, will play a key role in determining the ultimate benefit that the organization will derive from microcomputer use. Its responsibilities can include:

Establishing microcomputer software and hardware standards to meet overall organization information-system objectives.

Developing and presenting user-training programs to demonstrate to management and employees the benefits of microcomputer use.

Creating an awareness of security and control concerns and informing users of procedures needed to maintain adequate safeguards. This is extremely important in light of the degree of user involvement required to create an effective microcomputer-control program.

Acting as a technical consultant to users.

Maintaining a software information center that provides a directory of applications available within the organization. This will help prevent duplication of effort and waste of corporate resources.

Monitoring technological advances in both hardware and software to inform current and potential users of available offerings, as well as to determine the possible effect of these changes on the organization's information system. The adequacy of existing security and control procedures should also be reviewed as changes occur.

The active involvement of management in the integration of microcomputers into an organization should lead to the establishment of a sound control environment. It should also provide invaluable to the organization's success in maximizing the benefits of what may prove to be one of its most powerful resources.

SUMMARY OBSERVATIONS

> Microcomputer proliferation results in widely dispersed programming activity, scattered processing, and decentralized data storage.
>
> Adequate security and control for microcomputers require both user involvement and data-processing leadership.
>
> The changes brought about by the microcomputer environment increase the number of employees and outsiders possessing both the opportunity and skill to commit computer-related improprieties.
>
> Identifying exposure, determining risk, and selecting policies and controls are activities that are as important for microcomputer applications as for mainframe applications.
>
> Management should establish a microcomputer support function to oversee organization-wide microcomputer activity, such as establishing standards and training programs and creating an awareness of security and control.

5

THE VITAL LINK
An Effective Internal-Audit Group

As with your other policies, EDP policies should be monitored to evaluate effectiveness and continuing relevance. A clear understanding that top management and directors insist on and monitor adherence to policies and procedures encourages compliance. Typically, policymakers rely on several groups to monitor or review their policies: steering committees, data-security groups, and outside auditors and consultants. A vital link, though, is an effective internal-audit department.

In many companies, the internal-audit group plays a leading role in ensuring that management's EDP policies are working. The blend of accounting, auditing, and data-processing abilities possessed by a qualified group places internal audit in a unique position to evaluate the control implications of new or modified systems. Internal auditors' examination programs should be designed to test compliance with established accounting-related computer controls and to identify over-controlled situations, as well as control weaknesses and procedures in need of change.

Auditing is changing rapidly in today's highly computerized environment. New audit approaches designed to test computer-based controls and retrieve information that may be available only in electronic form are being implemented in response to sophisticated accounting and information systems. Auditors now focus on computer-based records as they once focused on manual records and hard-copy audit trails. Little wonder that data-processing professionals are dealing with auditors more frequently than in the past.

To be effective in an EDP environment, your internal auditors should be capable of designing tailored programs to test EDP performance, be conversant with industry-standard techniques for testing the reliability of programs and be able to use available computer-assisted audit-testing (CAAT) software, such as generalized retrieval and report-writer programs. In the interests of efficiency, internal auditors should be using the computer to: sort, retrieve, compile, and analyze transactions for audit testing, including sampling and exception-basis review; perform original computations for audit purposes; and reperform computations in order to test the proper functioning of computer programs.

INVESTING IN EDP AUDIT CAPABILITIES

An internal-audit group that possesses computer-audit capabilities is not only an asset but a necessity in most computer-dependent organizations. Management should ensure that, in addition to having the requisite technical skills, the internal-audit group has direct access to top management and directors. This promotes the group's independence and ensures that internal-audit recommendations receive prompt attention. An effective internal-audit group requires the confidence and respect of user and EDP management. The internal auditors must be provided with resources consistent with their assigned responsibilities.

The cost of maintaining a quality audit program has risen along with the level of sophistication of automated systems. This increasing cost not only reflects escalating salary, training, and other expenses; it also represents management's increasing commitment to establish and maintain quality computer-based and other control systems. The cost of not implementing sophisticated control systems in today's computerized environment can be substantial.

As with any business matter, there is a cost/benefit decision associated with expansion of EDP-auditing capabilities. Policymakers must be concerned with maximizing the benefits derived while controlling total cost. How can you tell if your internal auditors are at the minimum threshold necessary to be effective contributors to your control environment? Some questions worth asking are:

> Do your internal auditors actively participate in the development of new computer systems for the purpose of recommending controls necessary to minimize computer processing risks?
>
> Is the technical competence of your internal auditors adequate and do they communicate effectively with your computer professionals?
>
> Are internal-audit techniques as advanced as your EDP systems?
>
> Are you committed to a program of professional education in computers for your internal auditors? What outside courses have they attended? How do these courses compare to the courses taken by your EDP professionals?

RESPONSIBILITY FOR MONITORING

The internal-audit group provides management with information about compliance with policy and with recommendations for changes. Management—not the internal auditors—should establish policy. Ultimate responsibility for establishing strong control systems—data processing and otherwise—lies with executive management and the board of directors. The auditing function is a basic feature of the overall control system; it serves to give assurance to management that all other controls are functioning as intended.

For example, management needs to have adequate information to enable it to manage the business. It delegates the responsibility for developing quality information resources to users and computer professionals, such as the data-processing or MIS director. Computer professionals are also given the responsibility for instituting the controls necessary to ensure that an organization's information is adequately protected from misuse. Departments that use data have responsibility for instituting adequate controls at the application level.

It is the auditor's responsibility to review the adequacy and effectiveness of all controls put in place so that assurances about their design and effectiveness can be provided to management. The goals of the data-processing professional, the users of data, and the auditor are not—or should not—be in conflict. They all share the goal of solid, cost-effective controls. In a healthy environment, all parties should work together to satisfy mutual goals: ensuring that the organization's information is protected from misuse.

AUDITOR'S OBJECTIVES

The auditor, in attempting to meet responsibilities related to computer-based systems, focuses attention primarily on the following areas: the adequacy of specific application controls, the adequacy of general or pervasive controls (for example, whether incompatible functions have been segregated), the adequacy of data-security features, and the adequacy of disaster-recovery procedures.

It is central to the auditor's approach that he or she understand fully that the business environment is not static, that effective controls may become outdated or ineffective because of changes in circumstances. Because controls are dynamic, it is necessary to repeat review procedures periodically to determine whether unplanned and unmanaged changes in the control environment have occurred.

What are the auditor's motives? Why is the auditor interested in various aspects of computer-related controls? How does the auditor go about testing these controls?

Despite the manual effort, paperwork, and inefficiency of the older manual systems, they did have the advantage of leaving a clearly defined trail for the auditor and being relatively inexpensive to improve. Auditors typically selected transactions and reviewed the underlying paperwork to ensure that the control systems were operating properly. Early computer-based systems maintained the paper trail; auditors often monitored such systems by ignoring the computer and auditing much the same as they always had. As a practical matter, these older audit approaches often are no longer possible.

To determine the effectiveness of controls that are now embedded in computer software and the accuracy of transactions that are recorded electronically, auditors have developed new and different audit approaches. They must ascertain that effective "invisible" computer-based controls are in place and that these controls are functioning properly. Processing test data, for example, is a procedure whereby the auditor designs and processes sample transactions to see whether the system accepts or rejects different transactions. This procedure enables the auditor to confirm the existence or absence of programmed controls in the application system. By processing a comprehensive set of such transactions, the auditor can be assured that application controls function effectively and error and exception reports are appropriately inclusive.

Integrated test facilities are similar in concept, but test routines are actually embedded in the application system to capture and test transactions, which are often "live" transactions. Another audit approach may be for the auditor to review the logic of the application software to determine if it functions as purported. This approach is usually used as a last resort because it is often the least cost-effective.

DATA SECURITY REVIEW

In today's rapidly evolving telecommunications environment, data security is of increasing importance and concern. It is essential that some information resources be maintained on a confidential basis since survival in the competitive marketplace may very well depend on your organization's ability to protect its trade secrets.

Given the importance of maintaining confidential information and the propensity of hackers to violate that confidentiality and/or destroy other critical data, it is little wonder that managers are looking to data-processing professionals and auditors for additional assurances that reasonable procedures are in place to protect the organization's information assets. Auditors recognize that a truly effective effort to control data security requires the dedication and interest of data-processing professionals.

The auditor has a broad-based knowledge of the organization's information systems and interrelationships between applications, and an external viewpoint as to what constitutes sensitive financial information. The data-processing professional has technical expertise pertaining to existing security-systems design, hardware, and software. Approaching the challenge of data security by combining the talents of these two professionals results in an effective utilization of resources.

The benefits of installing security measures designed to keep unauthorized individuals out of your organization's computer systems are clear. But we all recognize that properly designed data-security measures may make the overall system less efficient by restricting access of bona fide users. Practical trade-offs are required; auditors and data-processing professionals need to consider those trade-offs together.

Where else may internal auditors help? Disaster-recovery planning, like data security, is an area where the efforts and recommendations of auditors can result in a true service to the organization. A pragmatic approach by auditors to addressing the real and potentially pervasive risks of not properly planning for a disaster could save your organization substantial resources.

INTERDEPARTMENTAL COOPERATION

The data-processing department is often the most overlooked organizational resource available to help ensure the quality and effectiveness of the auditing effort. The special skills and experience already present in this department are assets, and they should be used to build and maintain the audit program. Although many people, including some internal auditors, view the monitoring and review effort as solely the auditor's responsibility, this approach is not appropriate if your organization's resources are to be most effectively utilized. Maximizing those resources requires a truly coordinated effort among several departments—and especially between data processing and internal auditing. Obtaining a better understanding of each other's goals and objectives is a good starting point.

A dialogue should be established between the internal-audit director and the data-processing director to assess your organization's specific audit objectives and to ensure that your auditors understand the goals established for the data-processing department.

Clearly, there are a number of steps that should be taken by both computer professionals and internal auditors that would have a positive effect on your organization's overall efforts to maintain a high level of computer-related controls. Some are obvious, others are more subtle. The following are some suggestions that might help computer and audit professionals more effectively fulfill their responsibilities.

Preaudit Meetings

Preaudit meetings should be held to ensure that objectives of the pending internal audit are understood. Computer professionals can contribute to auditor scope decisions by expressing concerns candidly. For example, a director's observations about controls and operations are extremely useful in reducing audit emphasis in areas of low risk and increasing audit focus in areas of higher risk.

Review Audit Reports

Avoid surprises by ensuring that data-processing people understand in advance who will receive the internal auditor's report. In areas relating to Management Information Systems (MIS), be sure the audit reports are reviewed by the data-processing or MIS department prior to finalization. This should increase harmony with the auditors and avoid situations where the auditor proceeds with a report containing an erroneous assessment of the EDP systems. Data-processing professionals should always review audit recommendations to resolve factual issues and to communicate their viewpoint before the report is finalized and distributed to top management.

Retrieval Software

Operations personnel and the internal auditor should review and evaluate the technical capabilities of audit-retrieval software to ensure that purchased packages can be fully utilized in the systems environment. They should determine what type of information the auditors obtain today and what information they would like to have, but don't. Perhaps internal auditors can use existing utility programs or query languages to extract the desired information. Providing data-processing staff to help develop automated-audit modules will save significant internal-audit effort and data-processing staff time over the long term.

Integration of Technology

Joint projects should be initiated to study and coordinate the effect of introducing new technology into the organization. Consider introducing interdepartmental-training seminars to help employees cope with these changes. For example, many organizations are now developing microcomputer guidelines, including policy and procedures manuals, and organizing employee-training seminars.

Systems Development

Make internal auditors an integral part of systems-development teams so that their recommendations for control enhancements are considered at the outset, rather than during systems modifications. This approach provides additional assurance that significant control issues are fully considered in advance so that costly, after-the-fact modifications can be avoided. Clearly, the need to involve internal auditors in the development and software-selection process is important and will provide the organization with significant long-term benefits.

Education Programs

As technology progresses, internal auditors will need to acquire many of the skills that computer professionals possess. Consequently, many training programs (in-house and otherwise) for computer professionals will also be of value to auditors.

Encourage camaraderie and professional interchange among internal-audit and computer professionals. Sponsor joint technical sessions to discuss evolving hardware and software technologies and their effect on your organization.

Technology Updates

As new technologies are introduced by vendors, data-processing professionals should share the information with audit personnel. Advise them whether new technologies are likely to be incorporated into your organization's systems and, if so, how they may affect existing controls and create or mitigate security risks.

Staff Exchange

Arrange for staff to participate in short- to intermediate-range projects or assignments in other departments as a means of improving complementary technical skills. This exchange will give staff a better appreciation of other departments' goals, objectives, and problems.

SUMMARY OBSERVATIONS

An effective internal-audit group is the link needed to ensure that policies are working well.

Developing a coordinated and cooperative effort among professional groups within an organization will help ensure that resources committed to monitoring compliance with policies are well-utilized.

Auditing is changing rapidly in today's highly computerized environment; new audit approaches are available and being implemented.

Management should ensure that it has made the investments necessary to provide internal auditors with requisite technical skills.

The goals of the data-processing professional, the users of data, and the auditor are not—or should not—be in conflict. Marshalling resources toward the common objectives of strong computer-related control systems and an efficient and effective monitoring function will require the skills of both internal-audit and computer professionals.

6

DATA SECURITY
Ten Tough Questions

In the past few years, an increasing number of policymakers have focused attention on computer-security risks and the responsibility to minimize these risks. Headlines highlighting serious security breaches demonstrate that this attention is warranted.

Computers are no longer limited to relatively routine processing activities, such as accounts payable and payroll. They are now integral to the overall operation of most businesses, affecting such areas as strategic planning, research and development, and manufacturing. The changing role of the computer in business demands that the executive assume a new role in addressing computer-related issues. Board and top management action will be concentrated in four areas:

Policymaking. Setting broad goals and standards

Responsibility. Assigning responsibilities for execution and supervision

Resources. Committing the necessary financial and people resources

Review. Providing appropriate mechanisms to measure progress and performance

How do you determine the extent of computer security already in place and identify those areas where additional actions are required? We suggest you start by asking the following questions:

TEN QUESTIONS

Have written corporate policies regarding data security been distributed to employees?

Management's expectations of data safeguarding must be clearly communicated to employees. Many computer-security violations are caused by users who simply do not understand the consequences of their acts. A good example is the misuse of passwords and ID numbers that is at the very heart of most data-security problems.

The recent explosion in the use of powerful microcomputers and communications links between microcomputers and corporate databases make imperative the widespread dissemination of data-security policies to all users. A recent survey by Price Waterhouse found that less than 50 percent of business organizations communicated these policies to users outside the data-processing area. (Please refer to the Appendix for additional information.)

Does a data-security function exist and to whom does it report?

Dispersion of responsibility for data security carries the risk that no one exercises real control over security procedures. Management should assign to one individual or group the responsibility for executing data-security functions.

The data-security function will usually report to an individual within data-processing operations during the period in which the function is developing; the need for the cooperation and support of the data-processing department is essential. Once the function has matured it should report to the top EDP/MIS official, or, in larger or more sophisticated computer environments, to the individual (Chief Executive Officer, Chief Operating Officer, and Chief Financial Officer, etc.) to whom the top EDP/MIS official reports.

Do internal auditors really have EDP auditing (including data-security review) capabilities?

For effective data security, the answer must be an unqualified yes.

Therefore, management should budget for and promote advanced EDP audit-training activities. Current state-of-the-art data-security courses should be required for those individuals auditing complex systems. With technology changing at breakneck speed, internal auditors should also attend technical computer courses to be sure they are keeping up with the technology they audit. Hiring internal auditors having a computer-oriented background (whether by academic training or by prior experience in a data-processing environment) and mandating continuing education are essential to effective computer security.

Are data-processing, data-security, EDP-auditing, and user departments working together or at loggerheads?
Computer security is difficult enough to accomplish when all departments are pulling together; it is impossible to accomplish in an atmosphere of friction and squabbling for turf. To avoid problems, management should ensure that:

> All departments review and approve new software applications to be sure that data security is considered before any new system is introduced
>
> Mutual professional respect is encouraged
>
> Seminars and internal technical-update sessions are attended by representatives of all user departments
>
> Career paths across departmental lines and staff-exchange programs are considered

Is there an adequate reporting system?
Actual losses and attempts at data-security violation should be reported to top management. Management must know the extent of losses and near-misses; reports on misuses of passwords and unauthorized activity by employees should not be buried in routine reports.

One question that should be addressed squarely and before the fact: Is the company prepared to prosecute all security violators? Making it clear that abusers of your computer pay the consequences may serve as a deterrent to computer crime.

Has a security-software strategy been established, and is it being followed?

In order to create effective and efficient data security in sophisticated computer environments, such as on-line systems, software-program controls should be implemented. Only in the last five to seven years or so has comprehensive computer software been available to meet this requirement for most computer systems.

Previously, organizations desiring security software were forced to either develop their own or settle for limited security features available through a number of unrelated software packages, such as program-librarian and network-control software. As technology changed and additional on-line access paths (such as timesharing terminals and microcomputers) were implemented, these "patchwork" security schemes became unduly complex and resulted in redundancies, inconsistencies, and gaps.

Security-software products now available cure a number of these problems; it is therefore important for management to develop a strategy to select and implement such software.

Is your data-security system active or passive?

Is your organization waiting for problems to be reported or aggressively meeting problems head-on? For example, if a hacker attempts to access ("attack") the computer system, does the security software used merely report, after the fact, that an unauthorized user tried and failed at such and such a time; or, does your system go into what is called an "extended dialogue" to keep the hacker on the telephone line while the company's computer operator is alerted to the problem? Does your computer disconnect a user after a specified number of violations, making it very time-consuming to guess a valid password? Does your organization review well-known hacker electronic bulletin boards to see if your passwords or other ID information are posted for the misuse of others? In today's computer environment, security demands more than lip service. Make sure your data-security program is an active, not passive, one.

Is the password and user-ID system serious or trivial?

It is one thing to have a password system or user-ID system installed;

it's another to take such a system seriously. For example, if passwords are easy to guess, why even bother with them?

In a serious system, passwords are randomly generated, changed often, and protected by password owners. Passwords are of sufficient length to eliminate guessing, and a user is disconnected after a few unsuccessful attempts to guess a valid password.

When were corporate data-security controls last reviewed by top management?

Your risk profile changes as your business changes and as the overall computer environment changes. Piecemeal looks at your system are not good enough. Is there a program for periodic top-level reevaluation of your data-security program—from both a policy and technical standpoint? Whenever significant business developments occur, computer security should be reexamined. For example, changes in the value of assets to be protected, a changing computer environment (major hardware or software changes), or integration of computer systems following a merger would certainly demand another look at computer security.

Is top management really interested in data security?

This question is the most important one. Management must have an interest in data security and support the efforts of data-processing professionals to establish sound security programs. It must commit the time to set corporate policies as well as the dollars and personnel necessary to get the job done.

It is easy to say that data should be safeguarded from accidental or deliberate disclosure, modification, or destruction. The issue to be addressed by management is not whether an organization should implement data security, but how far on the security continuum your organization needs to travel.

Computer-data security is composed of many layers, and is only as strong as its weakest layer. Management and data-processing professionals have implemented varying degrees of protection over EDP systems, generally based on ongoing cost-benefit considerations. Tough data-security measures may make the overall system less efficient and more difficult to operate by bona fide users. Practical trade-offs are necessary and must be determined by top decisionmakers.

ACHIEVING A BALANCE

The desired security balance will be achieved based on consideration of the following:

> The potential loss resulting from intentional or unintentional misuse of data: actual loss of assets, diversion of assets to unauthorized persons, embarrassment from publicity resulting from unauthorized access to your system
>
> The sophistication of data-processing environment (on-line access, use of dial-up communications network, use of database technology, wide access to system by a large class of users)
>
> The importance of computer systems in day-to-day operations

If your organization is like many dynamic organizations, your complex computer systems probably require improved security measures. Protecting corporate assets is too important to delegate to others. Are you receiving satisfactory answers to your computer-security questions?

SUMMARY OBSERVATIONS

> Headlines highlighting data-security breaches demonstrate that the risks and responsibilities are very real.
>
> Top-level action should be concentrated on four areas: policy-making, responsibility, resources, and review.
>
> Tough questions should be asked; the answers won't be black and white, yet they should provide a sense of direction.
>
> Computer security is composed of many layers, with security as sturdy as its weakest layer.
>
> Practical trade-offs between tough data-security measures and their costs are necessary and must be addressed by top decisionmakers.

PART TWO

UNDERSTANDING THE TECHNOLOGY

7

THE CHANGING LANDSCAPE

Over the past 30 years, rapid strides in technology have brought radical changes to business information systems. The armies of clerks who once processed information manually have been replaced by automated systems that provide speed, accuracy, flexibility, new service opportunities, and improved tools for decisionmaking. Best of all—and unlike almost everything else—the cost of computer-processing power is declining. Let's look at today's technology, but first, a look at how we got to where we are may be useful.

THE EVOLUTION OF TECHNOLOGY

Building on earlier mechanical and electronic devices, the first generation of commercially produced, general-purpose computers appeared in the 1950s. These early systems, using vacuum tubes for internal memories, and punched cards and magnetic tape for input and output of data, were much faster than the manual systems that they replaced. Still, they were extremely slow by today's standards. In addition, only a single program could be running in the computer's memory at one time and each program had to be executed before the next program could begin. Assembling similar data in "batches" for processing was a necessary step and writing programs in the programming languages of the day was a tedious and difficult chore. These languages bore little resemblance to the written word and were difficult to learn and use.

Transistors replaced vacuum tubes in computers introduced from about 1958 to 1964 and brought dramatic improvements in size, speed, reliability, and cost. Also, during this period, programming became easier with the introduction of more advanced system software to perform some internal computer functions and permit the use of easier-to-use high-level languages (i.e., closer to normal human languages), such as COBOL and FORTRAN. Although programs were still executed one-by-one in a batch mode, systems development was made more efficient by linking some programs to commonly used program subroutines. Magnetic disks and drums began to provide alternatives to magnetic tape for external storage of data.

The next computer-system advances arrived in several stages from 1964 to the early 1970s. Transistors were replaced by stratified layers of integrated circuits, again with dramatic improvements in size, speed, reliability, and cost. One key characteristic of these computers was the availability of new operating systems that made computers capable of processing more than one program at a time. This "multiprogramming" capability was combined in the 1970s with "virtual storage," where parts of programs are held in external storage until they are needed for processing, thereby making the computer's use of memory more efficient.

The availability of multiprogramming and virtual-storage features, along with advances in telecommunication links to the computer and more sophisticated vendor-provided teleprocessing software, allowed computer terminals to be widely used. Interactive "on-line" applications were a reality. These features allowed the computer to deal with a single transaction as it occurred and made computer services available simultaneously to multiple users located great distances from the computer facility. Sophisticated systems software was developed, such as database-management systems for managing large masses of data for multiple usage and data-communications monitors for coordinating the receipt of transaction data from telephone lines and other communications facilities to the central-processing hub.

WHERE ARE WE HEADED?

Certainly, hardware and software improvements will continue at a rapid pace, although recent advances have been evolutionary, without the more dramatic breakthroughs that clearly delineated the systems advances of the past. Many industry analysts believe that the next advances in computer systems will be distinguishable primarily by important advances in easy-to-use software rather than by significant changes in hardware. Advances probably will include: user-friendly software programs that help create additional programs, software better able to be tailored by users, sophisticated yet easy-to-use decision-support systems, and so-called artificial intelligence software that allows computerization of some human deductive-reasoning processes in certain situations.

As for hardware, machines are available today that operate 10 times faster, are 10 times smaller, and cost 10 times less than the most powerful computers of 1975. Indeed, performance projections indicate that improvements will continue at an increasing rate.

These dramatic improvements in hardware and communications price and performance have been accompanied by a trend toward easier-to-use computer software. New systems software designed for smaller computers and new data-retrieval programs for larger computers continue this trend. Further, employee computer literacy continues to increase rapidly as computer technology reaches homes, schools, and all parts of the office and factory. It is now common for computer novices to be using computer systems productively after only a few hours of self-training.

DATABASE-MANAGEMENT SYSTEMS

Common usage in recent years has tended to overwork the word "database." Broadly defined as "an assembly of related items of information," the word correctly describes either a simple mailing list or a complex set of data records continually accessed and updated through multiple-application programs. The following discussion, however, relates to the more sophisticated database environments, those requiring special skills and advanced software to build and maintain.

The main objective of using database-management software is to provide an efficient means of handling information needed by many different users, all of whom may be using different application programs requiring different views, or pieces, of the same database. Use of this software also includes the tools that expedite technical tasks related to development of programs and maintenance of existing programs.

Database software is used to define the relationship of the pieces of data and how they will be retrieved and updated by application programs. Because data is stored and managed by the database software independent of the application programs that use the data, either the programs or the data can be changed without disrupting the other. This data and program independence can greatly reduce the cost of maintenance. In a database, data elements or applications required by multiple users can be shared, thus eliminating the need to duplicate and store the same data in separate files.

The core of the database system is software called, appropriately enough, a "database-management system" (DBMS). The structure of data stored in a database system is completely different from that in the traditional system, which worked with separate files of data. Once properly installed, a database approach provides substantial flexibility when making system modifications. It may help reduce or eliminate data duplicated in separate files. Furthermore, use of a DBMS can provide an increased level of data security as the more sophisticated DBMS provides the tools to limit access to data.

With these advantages, why would any organization not use database technology? One straightforward reason is that the associated costs are not trivial. The costs of DBMS software, skilled EDP personnel required to install and maintain the database, and additional processing overhead may be substantial. The data-sharing feature of database technology adds to coordination problems. Decisions must be made as to which users "own" which data, who is responsible for accuracy and security of the data, and who is permitted to read and update which data items. Although similar decisions must be made in the more traditional environments, use of DBMS software significantly complicates the issues. Also, backup and recovery procedures are more complex than such procedures in traditional environments.

Frequently, installation of a sophisticated database system necessitates the appointment of a database administrator (DBA) with responsibility for the overall design and maintenance of the database and liaison with use departments sharing the system. In a large system, it is preferable that the DBA function be independent, not only of user departments, but also of computer operations, programming, and data-security functions. In very large systems with large numbers of inter-related data elements, several individuals may be assigned full-time to the DBA function.

There is clearly a strong trend toward the use of databases. The decision to install a database system, however, should be made only after senior management has been presented with the potential advantages, disadvantages, and realistic costs of such a system.

Installing and maintaining a database system is a complex and expensive job. Management must be aware that moving to database technology requires solid planning, user involvement, and computer resources. It should also be remembered that it is not necessary, and often not practical, to have a fully integrated database system that encompasses the entire organization. Databases can be split into smaller, more manageable segments based on your organization's requirements.

DISTRIBUTED PROCESSING AND SMALLER COMPUTERS EVERYWHERE

Easy-to-use, low-cost, yet relatively powerful small computers provided the vehicle for the distribution of data-processing functions, not only to remote locations, but directly into user departments. Many organizations have moved away from totally centralized processing and programming toward largely decentralized end-user programming, data entry, and processing.

This general movement toward "distributed" processing reverses the trend toward centralization of computer applications that took place in the late 1960s and early 1970s. During that period, many companies sought to control their rising computer costs by taking advantage of the economies of scale available with the larger and faster computers. Improved data communications at reduced costs made it practical to service remote locations from central data-processing facilities where management control over EDP could be better maintained.

However, the advantages of a centralized approach were countered by major disadvantages. For example, the distance between the central computer facility and users often caused problems in communicating user requirements and in implementing solutions on a timely basis. Also, centrally developed "common" systems were often inadequate for the divergent needs of a wide range of users within a single organization. Due to such factors, both distributed-processing and alternatives were sought.

What is a distributed-processing system? Stated generally, it is a system that comprises several computers, each capable of performing specific processing tasks independent of the rest of the system. Often spread geographically throughout the organization, these computers are linked by a data-communications facility (usually a leased telephone line). Typically, data is processed on the computer located at a remote site and the resultant information is compiled in summary form and sent to a central computer for final processing. Distributed processing also may be used for exchanging data. For example, an information database may be shared by many computers; more complex tasks may be automatically routed to the most suitable computer in the network; selected data may be forwarded automatically to another computer for additional processing.

Today, many organizations have some combination of both centralized and distributed systems. In some circumstances, control policies and the need to consolidate data dictate that centralized processing is preferable for some types of applications and that distributed processing has the edge for others. For example, payroll and accounts-receivable applications may be centralized, while an organization's inventory systems may be distributed.

THE MICROCOMPUTER EXPLOSION

The "personal" or "desktop" computer has moved quickly into the business environment. Microcomputer sales are running at a worldwide annual rate of several million units, with the business market accounting for the majority of sales dollars. Each department of your business probably already has several microcomputers.

Initially, microcomputers were used for unrelated, relatively simple tasks, such as performing "what if" calculations with department budgets. Often microcomputers were used for applications that were just not available on the mainframe system. With continued improvements in price and performance and the rapid development of practical microcomputer applications software, micros have become integral parts of information-processing resources in many companies. Microcomputers are being linked to form networks for sharing resources, such as printers and external disks, and are being connected to larger computers by teleprocessing. (Consider the earlier discussion of distributed processing and databases.) Microcomputers are now being used as small general-purpose computers in distributed-processing systems, including systems that process accounting transactions and manage databases.

The distinctions between mainframes, minicomputers, and microcomputers are becoming less precise and may be misleading. For example, some of today's "microcomputers" are capable of processing more data in a shorter period of time than some "mainframes" of ten years ago. For this reason, these terms are used infrequently in the remaining chapters and only when necessary to illustrate a point that cannot conveniently be made otherwise.

SUMMARY OBSERVATIONS

Every advance in solid-state technology has resulted in smaller and more powerful machines. The computer chip promises to become even more powerful. Greater and greater power at lower and lower costs can be expected.

Continuing dramatic improvements in computer price and performance and the availability of easy-to-use application software to store and retrieve data, as well as to perform calculations, make it likely that your reliance on computer-based systems will increase.

Many believe that the next advances in computer systems will be marked primarily by important advances in easy-to-use software.

Improved data communications and the availability of small but powerful computers have made distributed processing a practical alternative to the centralized system, but have increased the need for strong management policies related to systems planning and development (including processing controls) and computer operations.

Database management systems provide a flexible means of handling data, but, because they are complex, they can be both costly and difficult to install and maintain. With the ever-increasing need to develop complex, on-line systems, proper DBMS planning and control are becoming more and more necessary.

Microcomputers and other small yet powerful computers have the potential to offer low-cost personal computing and electronic office facilities to staff within the organization.

More and more computer-literate personnel, more and more computers, and increasingly interdependent data-base systems in organizations without proper control tend to increase the level of computer-related risks.

8

WHAT ALL THESE COMPUTER PEOPLE DO, AND WHY

To recognize the risk implications presented by different organizational structures and methods, financial management must understand the functions typically performed in departments directly responsible for the management, development, operation, and support of computerized systems. Let's look at each as a means to appreciate what the computer professionals really do in your organization.

EDP STEERING COMMITTEE

Achieving effective communication among groups in your organization is essential to promoting the best use of computer technology. An EDP steering committee is designed to bring together computer professionals, users, and management to establish EDP priorities in the context of overall business objectives. In a large organization, it is a formal committee; in a small organization, a steering committee may be informal.

The committee must temper—with the realities of limited company resources—the natural but sometimes overly optimistic reactions of EDP management to new hardware and software announcements and the familiar cry of users that their new applications or projects are "most important." A steering committee can help balance several considerations, including allocation of limited capital and human resources, and relative importance of user requests.

The typical steering committee should have the responsibility and authority to adjust short-term priorities as required and to establish long-range EDP plans, including hardware purchases, subject to policy-level approval. Generally, the committee should meet at least quarterly.

Although the day-to-day operation of the EDP department is, of course, the responsibility of a professional EDP manager, the committee should consider providing specific, measurable objectives. General directives, such as to improve productivity, to reduce employee turnover, or to minimize capital investment, should be avoided. Instead, senior management and the steering committee should consider giving EDP managers tangible benchmarks for measuring performance, such as the number of program-change requests handled, the mean terminal-response time, batch-processing turnaround time, and actual EDP expenses versus budget.

ORGANIZATION AND MANAGEMENT

Computer organizations (or "shops") can, of course, range in size from one individual using acquired software on a small computer to hundreds of people using sophisticated software to operate computer networks with many machines of varying sizes. Many organizations process all data at a central-processing site. Reductions in hardware costs and improvements in data-communications technology and services have made it increasingly attractive for organizations to geographically disperse their computerized systems, either through use of decentralized processing or distributed data processing.

From the policymaker's standpoint, the type of system structure in use can have significant implications. For example, in a centralized structure, there is a single set of systems and application software in use. But in decentralized and distributed data-processing systems, each computer can have its own application programs and operating system. In these environments, data-processing management must be concerned with the adequacy of development and change procedures at multiple locations. Even if policy dictates the use of identical systems and procedures at every location, management must consider whether policies and procedures are being applied consistently at all locations.

Another issue that is affected by the type of processing environment is segregation of duties. Often, the number of data-processing staff at a processing site, especially those using small computers may be less than is desirable to provide for adequate segregation of duties.

No matter what system structure is in place, data-processing operations usually share certain common organizational and management features. For example, overall responsibility for planning, organizing, directing, and controlling data-processing activities is generally the responsibility of one individual. Of course, depending on the organization, this individual's title may vary (e.g., manager of data processing, information-systems manager, information-management director, vice president–information management). Where this individual (and thereby the data-processing department) fits within an organization's reporting hierarchy also will vary.

Historically, computers have most frequently been used to process accounting and financial data. As a result, the individual responsible for computers has traditionally reported to the chief financial officer or a delegate. Another approach is to view information as a corporate "resource" and computerized systems as management-information systems (i.e., systems for processing any type of information that may aid management in making decisions, irrespective of whether the information is financial in nature). Computerized systems have, under this approach, increasingly been moved from the purview of financial officers to the purview of operating officers.

Regardless of who has the ultimate responsibility for computerized systems and where they fit within the organization, the important point to consider is that data-processing management, working with the organization's top management, is responsible for planning, organizing, staffing, directing, and controlling the data-processing function. The quality of management can directly influence the quality of the data-processing control environment and, therefore, the reliability of financial and operating information. Sound management provides the obvious benefit of ensuring that data-processing activity is efficiently performed and that the department is appropriately funded to enable the effective performance of responsibilities.

An important role of departmental management is to create and maintain an appropriate control environment. If employees perceive that department managers only give lip service to controls, they will likely not place an appropriate level of emphasis on control matters. Obviously, management should be alert to situations where the design of segregation of duties seems appropriate, but where the existence of lax operating practice may allow employees to shortcut procedures. More directly, management's role is also to effectively monitor and supervise the department's activities and to ensure that employees at all levels adhere to established controls and that operating procedures are implemented to enforce those controls.

Another responsibility of departmental management is to ensure that hiring and training standards are appropriately balanced with the level of importance of employee responsibilities. Because of the pervasive negative effect that employee fraud or sabotage can have on the organization's operations, high standards should be established for hiring and investigating new employees. Special termination procedures should be established to ensure that employee privileges (such as passwords, keys, security passes, and so on) are revoked immediately on termination.

The size of an organization may have little to do with the type or sophistication of its computer systems. For example, depending on the nature of its business, a small company may have a large, complex, distributed system although a much larger company may have a small, centralized system. For this and other reasons, it is not possible to describe an organizational plan that will perfectly fit every organization; Figure 3, an organizational chart, is used as an example only to show the different functions generally performed in a data-processing department.

CHANGES THAT MAY AFFECT THE ORGANIZATIONAL STRUCTURE

Just as attitudes relating to the placement of a computerized system within an organization are evolving, so are attitudes regarding the organizational structure of data-processing operations. Figure 3 depicts the organizational structure of a data-processing department that

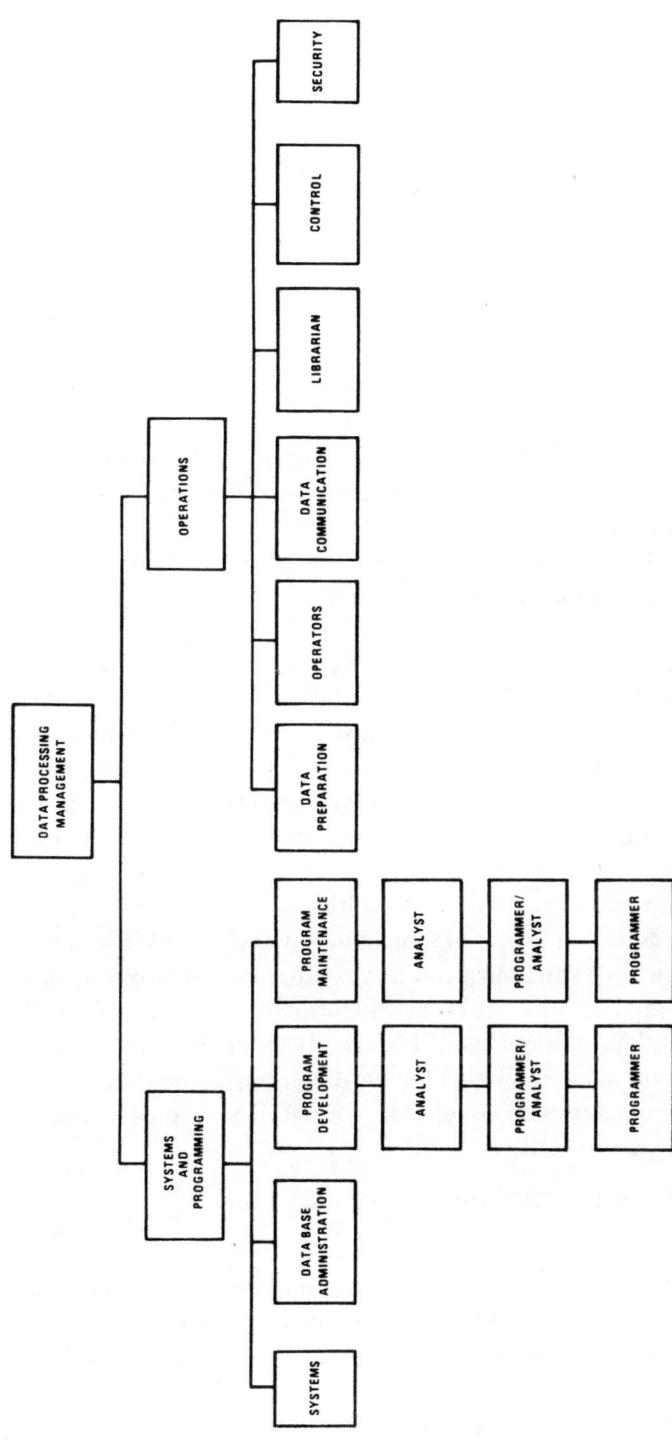

FIGURE 3. Example of Data Processing Organizational Structure

uses sophisticated hardware and software; one that is fairly typical in today's environment. As organizational theory as well as hardware, telecommunications, and software technology continue to progress, organizational structures will change.

In recent years, an approach to developing new systems has evolved that lets the user have greater responsibility in meeting his or her own needs. Many organizations have established what are commonly known as *information centers.* The information center, generally established as a division of the data-processing center, gives authorized users a direct (but, ideally, controlled) on-line connection to the organization's databases. By employing user-friendly software (such as, report writers or fourth-generation languages) to develop their own applications and generate their own reports, users can often get some of the information they need without going through the time-consuming and often costly process of more formal systems-development approaches.

The use of the information-center concept gives rise to additional concerns with respect to ensuring the integrity and security of an organization's information. In addition, multidepartment and large-volume applications may not be well-suited to this approach. The information-center concept offers more promise as computer literacy increases among users and as organizations capture, organize, and control data as a valuable asset.

Organizations with relatively sophisticated systems would generally have additional layers of management and supervisory personnel as well as further specialization in the programmer, analyst, and operations functions. Conversely, organizational structures of small data-processing departments would normally need few levels with less specialization at each level. There are two basic functional categories below the management level into which all data-processing department duties are usually classified:

Systems and programming

Operations

Simply put, the *systems and programming function* has responsibility for systems development and systems changes, while the *operations function* is responsible for day-to-day processing.

Both of these primary functional areas may be further divided into subgroups. Job titles and the responsibilities that go with them can and probably will vary from one organization to the next. The focus should be, not on job titles, but on the underlying duties that the individual(s) perform or have the opportunity to perform.

SYSTEMS AND PROGRAMMING

Systems and Programming Manager

The manager of systems and programming works with management to prioritize projects to meet the overall information needs of the organization. This individual plans, coordinates, and controls activities of those responsible for systems programming, the database administration (if applicable), applications programming, and maintenance.

Systems Group. The systems group is typically the most technically trained group in the data-processing department. Its responsibilities include effective maintenance and efficient operation of the systems themselves, hardware and software planning, and evaluation, maintenance, and modification of software obtained from outside vendors.

Systems software is used to facilitate the operation of the entire computer system, as opposed to the application software that is used to process transactions and information in accordance with requirements of particular users. Systems software includes the operating system, utilities, on-line editors, the file-access method or database-management system, and security software.

Systems programmers usually possess the technical skills necessary to make changes to low-level program code, such as assembler code. Most organizations with large computer systems will have at least one and typically a number of systems programmers.

The responsibilities of systems programmers usually require that they have access to systems-utility programs and on-line editors. These powerful tools can be used to make changes to programs and data without creation of a "audit trail." Accordingly, the circumstance where the use of these programs is permitted should be carefully controlled and monitored.

Security software can be programmed to restrict use of these tools and to automatically create an activity log each time they are used. Such a log should be used to facilitate supervision of the activities of systems programmers. Each unusual access to the system should be thoroughly investigated.

Under all but emergency situations, systems programmers should not be allowed access to source-code versions of application programs and date, program documentation, or other details of the processing functions of application software. Access to such information may place them in a position to more readily manipulate processing. Emergency procedures should be well-defined and appropriate audit trails created and reviewed.

Database Administration

An organization using database technology typically has multiple users of the same data. In these situations a database-administration group is generally responsible for the definition, organization, design, and efficiency of the database in use depending on the division of duties between database administration and data security. The database administrator may also be responsible for defining the rules by which data is accessed and stored. The individual who heads this group is generally referred to as a *database administrator (DBA)*.

Maintaining the integrity of data in a database (by fulfilling the responsibilities referred to in the preceding paragraph) requires the establishment of specialized procedures. The DBA's responsibilities also include the control of the database-management system software and the control of access and changes to the contents of the data dictionary/directory system.

Application-Systems Group

Members of the application-systems group work with user departments to analyze needs and design and develop computer programs to fulfill those needs. Members of the group, such as systems analysts, programmer/analysts, and programmers, usually work in teams under the supervision of a project leader. Each team member is responsible for a different phase of application development.

Systems analysts. They work closely with users in defining problems and/or opportunities for application systems. They evaluate alternatives, make recommendations for meeting user needs, and develop general system design for the selected alternative.

Programmer/Analysts. They are responsible for developing detailed computer program specifications based on the more general design provided by systems analysts. *Programmers* then take these detailed program specifications and code the instructions; compile and test the programs; write documentation for users, operations personnel, and the maintenance group; and test the new system.

Program-Maintenance (Change) Group

This group, which is often part of the application-systems group, is responsible for making repairs, modifications, or enhancements to existing programs. Depending on the size of the project, changing a program may involve the same steps necessary for new application development (i.e., problem definition, analysis, design, and so on).

Persons with responsibility for designing and developing application software have a detailed knowledge of the processing functions of that software. Accordingly, they should be prohibited from operating the computer. Further, they should not have access to production programs, job-execution statements (JCL) and data files used for production processing.

Separating the functions of development and maintenance from operations reduces opportunities to directly or indirectly influence the reliability of information contained in the organization's data files by affecting the execution of programs during processing. Special operating procedures can be designed and library-management software can be used to help ensure that these functions are effectively separated. Library-management software is discussed later.

OPERATIONS

Operations Manager

This individual is responsible for seeing that day-to-day operations are properly carried-out. This would typically include controlling and coordinating the activities of the staff responsible for data preparation, operations, and control.

Data-Preparation Group

The data-preparation group is responsible for the conversion of data into machine-readable form using devices such as microcomputers, visual-display terminals (CRTs), key-to-disk and tape devices, optical-character readers (OCRs), voice-recognition devices, and key-punch machines. Generally, when data is entered in an interactive mode by persons in user departments, fewer data-processing department staff will be involved with data preparation, as this function will have shifted to user departments.

Control Group

Establishing a control group may be necessary in certain environments to provide an adequate segregation of duties. Major functions include:

> Receiving input from users, scanning it for reasonableness and completeness and checking control totals
>
> Sending input to data preparation/operations
>
> Collecting source data and machine-readable data after data preparation has been completed and checking to see that all data required for the production run has been prepared
>
> Collecting output and machine-readable data from the operations group (after the production run), scanning output totals for completeness and to identify obvious errors, and returning output and source data to users

The data-control function has generally diminished in importance because a greater number of systems now use interactive data entry (rather than the noninteractive data entry that is more common in older, delayed-update processing systems). Accordingly, the data entry/correction function has been distributed to user departments.

Computer Operations Group

The computer operations group is responsible for maintaining computer operations, monitoring systems performance, responding to messages from systems software and application software (such as mounting tapes and changing papers as requested by the operating system), and coordinating the mix of jobs for submission to the computer to achieve efficient and effective use of the equipment.

Computer operators should be prohibited from making program and file changes and from having access to the source-code version of programs and related documentation. Because these individuals have physical access to the computer, security software must electronically prevent access.

Automatic job-scheduling programs or automatic-scheduling features of operations-management software can be implemented for purposes of reducing the control the computer operator has over processing. This reduces the risk that unauthorized processing activity can be initiated intentionally or unintentionally by the operator.

Data-Communications Group

This group is responsible for ensuring that proper communications facilities are available for use by the organization. This would include evaluating, implementing, installing, and operating communications controllers, data-transmission protocols, and communications networks. Once equipment is in use, members of this group have responsibility for monitoring and maintaining it. They also assist in correcting problems that may occur in data communications.

Librarian

The librarian function is responsible for maintaining and controlling an installation's physical library of data, JCL, and program files. The two major duties of the librarian are: (1) to ensure that files (program, JCL, and data) are used only for the purposes intended and (2) to maintain the storage media. The file-librarian function ensures files are checked out to computer operators as necessary to perform scheduled processing runs.

More and more organizations are now storing program and data files on nonremovable disks, making them essentially on-line at all times. This increases the importance of the library-management function. If not well-controlled, the production versions of application software and data files can be accessed by anyone using the system.

The librarian function is likely to be performed by two computer programs: *operations-management software* and *librarian-management software*. Operations-management software (including security software) can be used to control access to tape and disk files. The most important function of librarian-management software is to control the status of production programs and the recompilation and link-editing of source-code versions of application programs after changes have been made.

Data-Security Group

The increasing use of more sophisticated information systems has led to the evolution of a specialized data-security function. Generally, there are more opportunities to gain unauthorized access to these newer systems. The *data-security officer* (DSO) is responsible for the formulation of overall corporate policy relating to data security, data privacy, and the protection of data-processing facilities from events such as vandalism, theft, and misuse (this may include disaster-recovery planning).

In addition, data-security personnel are usually responsible for implementation and monitoring of operating policies and procedures to ensure data security, including authorization of new users, control of passwords, and monitoring of security-violation reports generated by security software. The DSO should be trained to identify indicators of unusual or unauthorized processing activity or access attempts, and to respond in a specified manner.

Data-security personnel should have sole access to security-code files but should not have access to equipment or production files; that is, the data-security function is a staff function and should not involve day-to-day computer operations.

It is easy to say that data should be safeguarded from accidental or deliberate disclosure, modification, or destruction. But it is often difficult to ensure that adequate safeguards exist. The first step is to define the procedures for your data-security function and to clearly assign one individual or group the responsibility for executing them. A dispersion of responsibility for data security carries the danger that no one exercises real control over security procedures.

Important concerns of the data-security function are to ensure that data is accepted for processing only from authorized sources and is processed using appropriate software. When computer resources are accessed from remote terminals, data-security personnel should review printed reports of rejected access attempts and investigate suspicious entries.

OUTSIDE CONSULTANTS

Internal auditors and your EDP professionals are often in a position to identify risks that need to be addressed. Recommendations of these groups or user groups may lead management to the conclusion that a review of parts of an EDP system is needed or that the entire computer-services area can benefit from a diagnostic-type review.

If your organization is fortunate to have adequate internal staff, a detailed review of the area of concern might be performed by your own personnel; or management might decide to employ outside consultants to assist your people and to provide an objective evaluation of the situation, including recommendations of what action, if any, is needed. Examples of work you may wish to have outside consultants perform include:

Data-security review to analyze the risks and develop the compensating procedures for establishing effective management control in several areas: organizational structure, authentication/authorization of transactions, data integrity, physical security, and data communications

Feasibility studies to determine if an automated solution for a problem is appropriate in terms of costs and benefits

Requirement-definition projects to prepare a complete and explicit description of the functional requirements and processing features that must be provided by a computer system in the specific operating circumstances

Hardware and software evaluation studies to assist in selecting the hardware and software capabilities most appropriate for the users' requirements

Reviews of overall computer-system effectiveness focusing on key areas of data processing, including organization and administration, personnel development, computer operations, data capture, hardware and system software, and application software

Long-range information-systems planning studies that consider business strategies, emerging technologies, user needs, the current state of automation, budgetary constraints, and personnel resources

Office-productivity management studies to suggest productivity improvements possible with more modern office systems, including service-group realignments, revised procedures and improved workstations

This list demonstrates the variety of computer-related assignments many consultants are prepared to offer. Before engaging outside consultants, make certain that both the consultants and senior management clearly understand the scope and objectives of the study, the relative roles of the consultants and internal staff, the results expected, and fee arrangements. Responsible consultants will insist that the parameters of their work be clearly defined in writing. Remember that the consultant's role is generally to gather relevant facts, to evaluate conditions found, to present alternative solutions, and to make recommendations for action by the organization.

Management, not the consultant, should, of course, make the final decisions on what actions, if any, are best for the organization. Data-security groups, internal auditors, steering committees, and outside consultants are most effective when working under the direction of interested and concerned senior management. Computer risks are not reduced by delegation, but by management participation in establishing and implementing policies. Management must set the tone.

SUMMARY OBSERVATIONS

> An active computer steering committee comprised of computer professionals, users, and general management is an effective means of translating business objectives, limited resources, and user requests into EDP priorities.
>
> Increasing user sophistication coupled with improved technology is clearly creating a more user-driven systems environment. The days when users were content to submit a request for a new report and wait months for its development are rapidly disappearing.
>
> Decreasing hardware costs and increasing capacity of small computers are resulting in a proliferation of computers within organizations. The body of thought that emerges relative to networking large numbers of units and using stand-alone applications will affect the organization of most computerized systems.
>
> Responsibility for data security should be specifically assigned. Designation of a data-security officer or group is often helpful.
>
> Outside consultants can supplement the efforts of your organization's computer professionals and provide you with an objective evaluation of your systems' performance.

9

DEVELOPING AND MAINTAINING SYSTEMS

Management must gain assurance that its computer systems are properly designed, tested, and implemented. An awareness of the procedures involved in developing a computer system should permit reasonable judgments on the likely quality of individual application systems that have been or are being developed. Management is seeing the need to become more involved in this area due to the relatively high cost of developing computer systems and their increasing importance on an organization's effectiveness, efficiency, and competitive edge.

SYSTEMS DEVELOPMENT: HOW SYSTEMS SHOULD BE BUILT

The systems development process can be described very simply as follows:

> User identifies a need.
> Analyst and user, working together, determine what must be done to meet that need.
> Analyst determines how it is to be done.
> Programmers build the software that will do it.
> Programmers and users test the software.

Data-processing, data security, and user departmental management approve the system.

Computer operations accepts and operates the system.

This is clearly a simplification of the steps involved with this key process. It is, however, the typical process that many organizations follow when developing computerized systems.

The importance of users and data-processing departmental personnel working together in this process must be emphasized. Systems-development projects will fail without sufficient user involvement. Some organizations help solve this problem by establishing a steering committee in the early stages of a systems-development project. These committees usually include representatives of the users' group, information processing, internal audit, and a higher level of management. The steering committee acts to oversee each phase of development and to review the implementation process.

In some organizations, the steering committee's charge is more general: to oversee the entire computerized information-systems function. In these situations, a standing committee of higher-level executives typically reviews and decides on user requests, establishes guidelines for systems development and implementation, reviews and monitors progress, and ensures that proper review and approval of new systems are obtained.

The investment of time, effort, and money connected with developing a new system is high and it is increasing. The effect that new systems have on an organization's success is also increasing. The bottom line: every organization should have established procedures for developing new systems. Procedures should be designed to ensure that systems are adequately planned, developed, tested, implemented, and controlled to ensure that they satisfy the needs of the user.

There are many acceptable systems-development methodologies in use. One example is the Price Waterhouse *System Management Methodology* (SMM), a comprehensive approach to computer-systems planning, development, implementation, and operations. SMM provides a set of standard activities/tasks designed for conducting a successful system-development project. Activities/tasks typically involved in applying this approach to systems development are:

Feasibility study
Requirements specification
Software-package evaluation
Conceptual-system design
System architecture
Implementation planning
Detail design
Program design
Program coding
Unit testing
System testing
Procedures and user documentation
Training
Implementation and system acceptance
Postimplementation review

Each of the activities/tasks included in the SMM approach to systems development is discussed in the following pages. The narrative explains in more detail the processes involved with developing a new system.

Feasibility Study

The feasibility study involves defining, on a conceptual level, one or more sets of business objectives of the organization and determining whether there are cost-effective data-processing solutions that can be used to meet those objectives. The primary dialogue during this phase of systems development is between the users and the information-processing department. Management and internal auditors also play a role in monitoring the decision processes supporting the conclusions reached. The result of this phase is a high-level implementation plan.

Requirements Specification

The purpose of the requirements-specification phase is to define the information requirements of the user. This is accomplished through the use of a uniform set of data-collection and analysis techniques. Although the primary onus to construct the list of requirements is on the users, the information-processing function typically assists them in doing this. During this phase, internal audit should be asked to determine that the user recognizes the importance of internal-accounting control as a critical success factor.

Additionally, the internal auditors can view themselves as users of the system in that applications can be constructed that include features primarily for their use. A good example is an embedded audit module included as part of the program code. Such a module could be used to capture all of a certain type of transaction (e.g., all invoices from certain vendors or payroll checks above a certain dollar amount) as they occur and to place them in a special file for later use by the internal or external auditors. It is helpful if features of this nature are considered as the system is being developed, because their addition at a later time will certainly be more expensive and may not be feasible.

Finally, a method for developing the system is chosen. The traditional method is for programmers to write program code; other methods discussed later in this chapter are to employ application-generation software or to acquire a software package.

Software-Package Evaluation

Software-package evaluation is an optional phase. It is undertaken if the requirements-specification phase indicates that a commercially available software package may meet a significant portion of user requirements. A vendor list is developed, requests for proposals are issued, and the responses are evaluated to determine which package best satisfies the requirements. At this time, any modifications to the package that are required will be identified. It is particularly important that control considerations be included in package-evaluation criteria because they usually cannot be added later.

Conceptual-System Design

During the conceptual-system design phase, processing requirements developed during requirements specification are organized into logical groups based on common input, output, and data usage. The overall flow of data is established and major subsystems and interfaces are identified. The design document that is developed during this phase should be written in terms that can be easily understood by both nontechnical users and management.

System Architecture

The objectives of the system-architecture phase are to: (1) develop a model of the system's data requirements (that is, define the data that the system is going to process and the relationships among that data); (2) prepare the preliminary layouts for input and output; (3) analyze the feasibility of distributed data processing (if this is a choice); (4) make preliminary estimates of network-communications requirements and related costs; (5) select an appropriate file structure; and (6) develop the logical database design, if applicable. At the completion of this phase, the architectural components from which the system will be built, how they might look, and how they might operate, will be defined. This will result in a functional system design.

Implementation Planning

Implementation planning should be an ongoing task throughout system development. It includes the development of a file-conversion strategy (the method for changing the old or manual system over to the new) and the definition of acceptance-testing criteria.

It is particularly important that control issues, such as proofing of converted files and data and testing of internal system controls, be considered during this phase.

Detail Design

Detail design includes the definition of physical input and output layouts, edit and validation requirements, system control and audit requirements, and procedures for restart and recovery in the event of a system failure. At the completion of this phase, all files, reports, and screens of the system are completely defined. These detail specifications should be carefully reviewed and approved by users, management, internal auditors, and the database administrator.

Program Design

The logic (the steps that should be taken and their sequence) of each application program is developed during the program-design phase. This phase should take place prior to program coding. The logic and processing flow should be documented at this time. The product of this phase is a set of comprehensive program specifications that state the program inputs, program outputs, and processing logic required to transform input to output.

Program Coding

During this phase, the computer programs that perform the automated processing functions of the system are written based on the designs developed during the preceding phase.

Unit Testing

The purpose of the unit-testing phase is to test each program in the system on a standalone basis to be sure that it functions according to the documented specifications. Unit-test plans are developed to test data formats, computational logic, and module interfaces. Each test plan should include the definition of test steps, test data, and expected results. The tests are then conducted, the results are verified, and problems are recorded and resolved. After any necessary changes, the tests are performed again. This procedure is repeated until all testing is satisfactorily completed.

System Testing

System testing involves the testing of all processing and procedural components of the system. The objective of this phase is to ensure that all functional specifications are operational, including user procedures, backup and recovery, and program-to-program interfaces. Whenever possible, the system test should be designed and conducted by an independent team. A detailed test plan should be developed that includes test conditions, test data, expected results, and user procedures. Problems should be logged, changes should be implemented, and testing should be redone as in the unit-testing phase.

Procedures and User Documentation

This phase should be conducted concurrently with the program design, program coding, and unit-testing phases. Its purpose is to develop user instructions for data entry, operation, review of output, and error correction. The accuracy, completeness, and clarity of this documentation should be verified during the system-testing phase.

Training

The training process includes training-materials development and training sessions. The review of system-generated audit trails and control totals should be included as a training topic.

Implementation and System Acceptance

During the implementation and system-acceptance phase the users should conduct tests to ensure that the system meets their specified requirements before they issue their formal acceptance. Such tests may include parallel operation of existing and new systems, processing of actual data through a specified number of production cycles, review of documentation, and analysis of system performance. The internal auditors should be involved in this phase to ensure that all system controls are functioning properly. When the system is finally accepted, it should be transferred into the production environment and all documentation should be submitted to the users.

Postimplementation Review

Several months after a new system has been accepted for production, a final review should be made by someone independent of the installation process to ensure that the system is achieving its intended objectives. This review is often performed by someone in the internal-audit department or in data-processing management.

Program Generation

There are several procedures that can be used as alternatives to certain phases of the SMM systems-development methodology, including program generation, prototyping, and application generation.

Program generation is an alternative to the program-design and program-coding phases. It involves the definition of program-processing requirements in a format so that they can be inputted to automated program-generation software. In other words, the user of program-generation software tells the program generator what the program is to do (the logic) and the program generator generates the program code (e.g., COBOL) to do it. It is important that control functions be included in the specification process.

Prototyping

Prototyping may be used as both an alternative to the requirements-specification phase and to produce an operational system. It involves the development of a working model of the system, beginning with a simple version illustrating input and output formats and progressing to more complex models that include editing and validation, security logic, and error processing. At each step in the development, the user is encouraged to experiment with the prototype. Changes are made based on the user's reactions. This phase may result in a fully documented set of user requirements and/or in a partially implemented but operational system.

An important benefit of prototyping is increased user ability to consider alternative approaches. A disadvantage is that the testing and documentation of the system are usually not as thorough as in the traditional approach. When should prototyping be used? When the user is not 100 percent sure of the system requirements and needs to see some alternatives.

Application Generation

Application generation is an alternative development approach that involves the definition of user requirements as input to automated application-generation software. Application-generation software is more sophisticated than program-generation software. Unlike the latter, where one program is generated at a time, application software will build an entire application.

Figure 4 illustrates the Price Waterhouse system management methodology. It shows the traditional development path (boxes with heavy black upper border), as well as the development paths that would apply if alternative techniques were followed.

SOFTWARE DEVELOPMENT BY END-USERS

Users are more frequently developing their own software, writing programs in relatively high-level languages (human-like languages). Sophisticated application-software programs are often used to create programs to perform specific tasks. Many commercial programs are becoming high-level programming languages in their own right, due to extensive use of "macro" or "learn" facilities and editing capabilities. Once tailored, these programs are used repeatedly in other users'

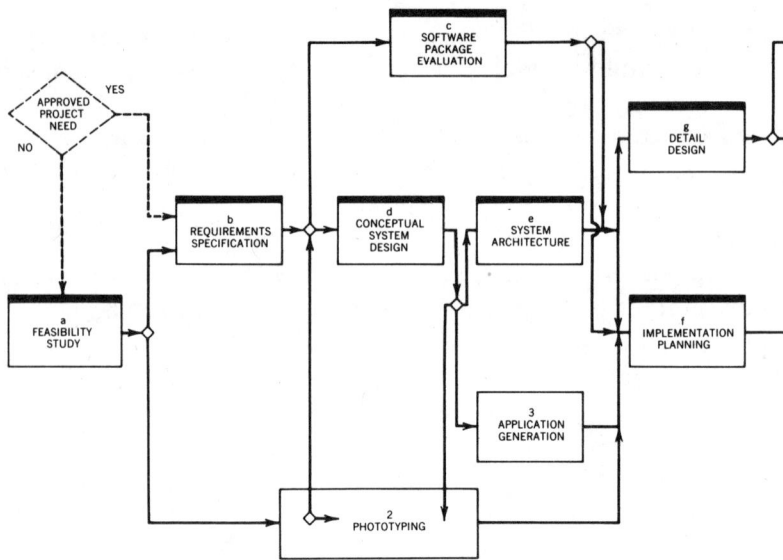

FIGURE 4. System-Management Methodology:

programs and may be, therefore, shared among several users. Also, fourth-generation retrieval languages are designed for users to create their own programs, primarily to obtain data entered, edited, and stored in database systems.

Software development can vary in focus and scope—from a simple template created with an electronic-spreadsheet program to more complex multiuser programs that are capable of concurrently performing complex tasks. Many users believe simple programs that are not shared do not require documentation or development standards. Wrong! The importance of documenting simple programs is highlighted when a change in responsibilities occurs. If a program is "simple," then it should be simple to document. Documentation and development standards should be taught to all users and enforced, as a matter of company policy.

Formalization of development activities is imperative for complex programs and those programs that will have widespread use within your organization. For such programs, the following should be clearly and concisely defined, documented, and approved:

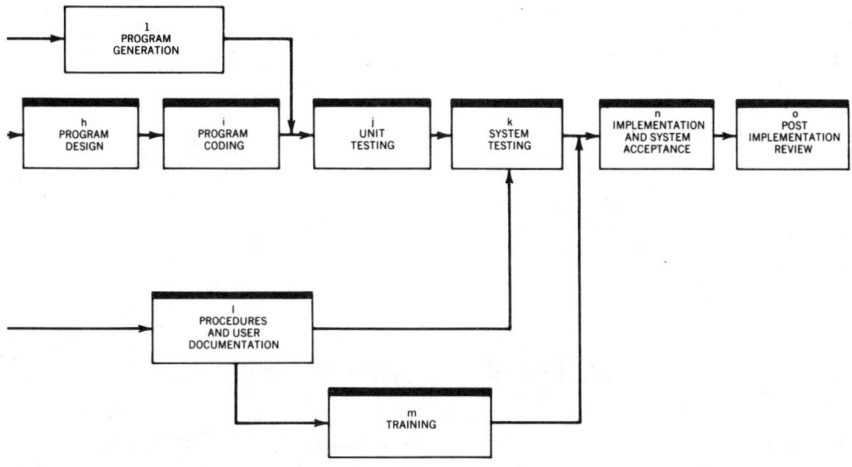

System-Development Paths

Objectives (the problem to be solved)
Conceptual system, program, or template design
Data-input requirements
Processing functions to be performed
Output requirements defined in terms of columnar headings to be presented on screens and/or printed reports
Key controls
Backup requirements and procedures

Documentation may be the most important part of software development. Effective documentation serves as a training aid for users, a technical-maintenance tool, and a permanent record of the programs. If documentation is poor or nonexistent, users will have difficulty using programs and maintenance of programs may be impossible. At a minimum, good documentation should include a description of what the program is intended to accomplish; the procedures, steps, and data necessary to use the program; and program or template coding.

Testing is also a very important part of software development. Programs often have "bugs" that affect the reliability of the program and related output in various situations. Whenever relatively simple programs are exchanged, each user should test the programs to ensure they accomplish their intended objectives. When more complex programs are exchanged, testing should be part of the formalized development process and completed prior to the release of the program for production use.

Audit and Management Trails

An audit trail, often referred to as a management trail, provides a means of identifying changes made to data files or actions taken during the processing of data. The design and use of most financial application software, such as electronic spreadsheets and databases, allow data to be easily modified without producing any audit trail. This lack of audit trail is often more a function of the personal nature and use of the microcomputer than a defect of any particular application-software package.

Audit trails are important in stand-alone microcomputer applications. For example, if an employee uses an electronic-spreadsheet program to calculate the company's earnings per share, the output of that calculation (and related formulas) should be detailed enough for adequate review and approval by a supervisor. This seems fundamental, yet in many instances, the importance of management review and approval has increased with the introduction of the microcomputer.

Small businesses are increasingly using microcomputers to maintain basic accounting records. Acceptable audit trails are imperative in these situations and can be accomplished by maintaining a log of activity, transaction counts, and balancing/batch totals. A summary of daily transaction activity (generated by the software program) should be balanced to totals developed independently by an employee other than the microcomputer operator. The balanced-transaction log should be reviewed and approved by an appropriate supervisor. Early accounting application software generally did not provide sufficient facilities for audit trails and balancing/batch controls; newer software usually includes these features.

CONTROLLING MAINTENANCE AND PROGRAM CHANGES

Due to the expense of developing new, or buying, packaged software systems, many organizations elect to repair and/or change, sometimes extensively, existing systems. Management concerns with respect to so-called patches are the same as those relating to the development of a new system: Does the system function as intended after modification and does the modified system have appropriate controls?

It is a conservative estimate that more than 50 percent of the programming time in most organizations is spent changing programs. Therefore, adequacy of an organization's software-change procedures, and the degree of consistency in their application, can have a significant effect on risks.

Program changes or "maintenance" activities include all efforts to keep software operational and adapt it to the changing environment and user requirements. Changes are generally made for the following reasons:

To correct errors in software

To adapt software in response to user needs as well as hardware, software, regulatory, and/or data-environment changes

To modify software to provide greater effectiveness and efficiency

An organization's procedures for modifying software should be well formulated, well documented, and well executed to ensure that programs operate as intended and modified software is not manipulated for unauthorized purposes during the program-maintenance process.

Procedures for making *major* software modifications should generally be the same as those used for new systems development (presented earlier). Procedures for all other modifications should include several steps. At a minimum:

Reasons for requesting modifications should be documented and approved by an appropriate level of management (for example, significant changes should normally require the same level of authorization as that for new systems development).

Changes should be made first to test versions of software, not production versions.

Changes should be made only by the systems and programming group (not by operations personnel).

Changes should be supported by adequate systems documentation.

Changes should be tested prior to being placed in production.

Documentation plays an important role in software maintenance. It assists the programmer who is called on to modify the program by providing that individual with a general description of what the program does, a detailed description of the workings of the program (program specifications), and a detailed description of the data going into the program and the resultant reports and displays produced by the system.

Testing of the revised software should first be performed by programmers (ideally by an independent test team). Testing should be designed to test for all possible conditions and should not be conducted by simply using a sample of live data. After the programmer/test team is satisfied with the revised system, the users should test the system to gain assurance that their needs have been met.

All changes should be reviewed and approved by a responsible individual independent of the programmer(s) who made the software modifications. A permanent record of all changes should be maintained. (*Note:* Librarian software can be used to automatically produce an audit trail of all changes made to software. This can facilitate the review process and provide the required record of change.)

Finally, the manager of programming/development should ascertain that coding changes have been reviewed and approved, and, along with user-department management, should approve the results of testing. Approval should be received prior to the placement of revised software into production.

When significant modifications are made to programs involved in processing accounting and financial data, the internal and external auditors may be required to revise tests of the system and the frequency with which some tests are conducted. If the format of master files has been modified and if the auditor uses auditing software in connection with testing those master files, revision of the auditor's program(s) may also be necessary.

SUMMARY OBSERVATIONS

Managers of computer systems, working with the organization's top management in areas such as departmental funding and long-range planning, are directly responsible for developing and maintaining an efficient, effective, and appropriately controlled data-processing environment.

Management may choose to use one or a combination of the three primary forms for structuring computer-processing systems: centralized, decentralized, and distributed data processing. The size of an organization may have little to do with the type or sophistication of its computer systems.

Regardless of the type or size of a data-processing department, it should be organized in a manner that maintains a distinct segregation of duties among data-processing staff. The three basic functional areas into which the duties of data-processing staff can be classified are: management, systems and programming, and operations.

Standard procedures for the development and maintenance of computer systems should be in place and followed. The procedures should provide for adequate evaluation, design, testing, and implementation of new systems and changes to existing systems.

Software developed by the user for small computer systems should adhere to documentation and development standards, albeit standards tailored to the user's environment.

10

HARDWARE
More Than You Need to Know About Nuts and Bolts

This chapter discusses hardware concepts and terminology used in contemporary computerized information systems. Common classifications of computers are: microcomputer, minicomputer, and mainframe. Conceptually, these machines perform identical internal computer functions, but on different scales. Peripheral equipment, such as disk devices, printers, and video screens, are also conceptually identical.

Basically, the bigger machines can do more things faster, often have and require better manufacturer support and service, and can generally accommodate a large number of users at the same time. Microcomputers have less capacity, require no special environmental protection (such as air conditioning), and, importantly, are relatively inexpensive. The power and price of minis fall somewhere between that of micros and mainframes. The border between high-end microcomputers and low-end minicomputers is blurred, as is the border between the more powerful minis and mainframes. The borders promise to become even more blurred. Further, the emerging technology necessary to link various sizes of computers promises to bring even more dramatic changes to the computer landscape.

Distinctions among various computers can be made in terms of:

Price ranges

Speed of internal calculations and input/output operation and volume of transactions

Size of files

Sophistication of software

Environmental requirements, such as air conditioning

Portability

Memory size (both internal and external)

Segregation of duties (operating, programming, and user functions are often combined in smaller systems, but are usually separate in mainframe-computer environments)

CENTRAL-PROCESSING UNIT

The central-processing unit (CPU, often called a "box") is the center of any computerized information system. It contains *main memory,* an *arithmetic-logic unit* and a *control section.* Each of these components is discussed in the following.

The major factors that determine how fast and in what quantities a CPU can process data are:

The size of its random access memory (RAM)

The number of instructions per second the computer can execute (often referred to as millions of instructions per second, or MIPS), which is related to the cycle time of the CPU

The speed of the *data channels* (explained later)

The number and size of data channels that can operate together

RAM chips are semiconductor-storage elements. They are tiny (almost microscopic) integrated circuits packaged on silicon chips that are often referred to as RAM chips because any of the storage locations (i.e., physical positions or addresses) on a chip can be used to directly store and retrieve data and instructions. Any of these locations may be written to or read from (accessed) in the same amount of time. When power to the computer is switched off (or fails), the data stored on most RAM chips is lost.

RAM chips are used to create the computer's main memory (also called *primary storage, real memory,* or simply *memory*). It contains a number of individual storage positions, varying from several thousand in very small computers to many millions in large machines. Each storage position is able to hold a given amount of data (e.g., a letter, number, or symbol, such as a comma or question mark). Because computers recognize only electronic impulses (i.e., an on/off condition), characters must be converted into electronic form to be read by the computer; that is, they must be made machine-readable. The process of converting characters into electronic representations is not fundamental to this discussion and we won't belabor the point.

Main memory is used to store two primary types of data: information and instructions.

Information includes that to be processed, that being processed (including that which is in an intermediate phase of processing), and that for which processing has been completed (prior to its release from the CPU).

Instructions specify what is to be done to information (e.g., how the computer program should process data).

Another type of storage element found in many CPUs is called a *read-only memory* (ROM) chip. ROM chips, usually supplied by the computer manufacturer as part of the system, are, in effect, preprogrammed memory. They are used to store fixed sets of elementary instructions, usually simple routines, for interacting with the computer system. The computer can read these instructions, called microprograms, over and over again from the ROM chip as needed. Unlike RAM chips, ROM chips will not accept any input data or changes from users. Also, ROM chips are nonvolatile. They retain stored data when the power goes off.

Two of the most commonly used codes for electronically representing characters in storage are the *Extended Binary Coded Decimal Interchange Code* (EBCDIC) and the *American Standard Code for Information Interchange* (ASCII). Both coding systems use a combination of 1s and 0s to represent characters. EBCDIC is used in many large computer environments. ASCII is used in computers of varying sizes.

SECONDARY STORAGE

Because main memory is volatile (will be lost when power is turned off) and relatively expensive, most data and programs are stored on secondary-storage media. Only those data and programs needed to perform a given task are brought into main memory from secondary storage at any one time.

The accessibility of data on secondary-storage media depends on the access type (i.e., direct or sequential access) and whether the medium being used for storage is physically connected to the CPU at the time it is needed. Access times can run as long as days in the case of backup reels of magnetic tape stored off-site, or as short as nanoseconds in the case of a direct-access magnetic disk connected to the CPU.

Storage media can be permanently connected to the CPU (always on-line), temporarily connected, or not connected (off-line). Physical connection is independent of the method of accessing the data after the medium is connected to the CPU. For example, a magnetic disk, which is a direct-access medium, can be stored off-site until its data is needed for an application. The trend is toward permanently installed storage devices.

Secondary-storage media are usually classified according to their access capabilities. *Sequential access* means that records are read in the order in which they are stored. For example, to read the fifth record on a magnetic tape, the previous four records must be read first. *Direct access* allows any one specific record in a file to be read without reading records before or after that specific record.

The direct access of data requires both a *direct-access storage device* such as a disk and a file-access software (e.g., virtual sequential-access method—VSAM) that provides for direct access. Otherwise, data must be accessed sequentially. Data can be accessed sequentially from any storage medium. Whether direct or sequential access is used generally depends on the percentage of the records in the file that are expected to be processed in a particular session.

The method of data access is only indirectly related to the timing of data processing. That is, if *immediate update* of transactions is desired, usually direct access, rather than sequential access, will be used. The converse, however, is not true. If *delayed update* is used, data access can be either direct or sequential.

There are several types of storage, including *magnetic disks,* the most popular form of direct-access storage. There are several types of magnetic disks, from very large magnetically coated disks that are mounted permanently in their cabinets, to mini-sized (generally 5.25 or 3.5 inches in diameter) *floppy disks* packaged in protective envelopes.

Mass-storage cartridge devices can store vast quantities of data that can be accessed directly. They consist of cartridges of magnetic strips wrapped around plastic cylinders. These devices are slow compared with disks, but are faster than magnetic tapes. The major users of mass-storage cartridge devices are organizations that need to access large amounts of information relatively quickly, such as insurance companies, banks, service bureaus, and governmental agencies.

Optical-disk systems use lasers to burn tiny pits into a thin coating on a disk. These pits are then read by other lasers. Data can be stored much more densely on this medium than on magnetic disk or tape. One small optical disk can store the same amount of information as 25 reels of magnetic tape, and the data can be accessed in milliseconds. Most commercially available optical-disk technology does not permit the data to be erased or changed after it has been written on an optical disk. For this reason the use of optical-disk systems is limited to applications that are largely archival or reference in nature. There are, however, efforts underway to create a technology for reusing this medium and several such systems have recently been announced.

Magnetic tape is a relatively low-cost medium (in terms of cost per volume of data stored). Data is read much more slowly with magnetic tape than magnetic disk. Data, stored as magnetized dots on one side of a tape, can be erased and the tape reused.

DATA-INPUT DEVICES

The process of on-line data entry involves several hardware and software components: data-entry devices, control units, data channels, data-transfer buses and main memory, including a buffer area. This flow of data is illustrated in the following diagram. The diagram and

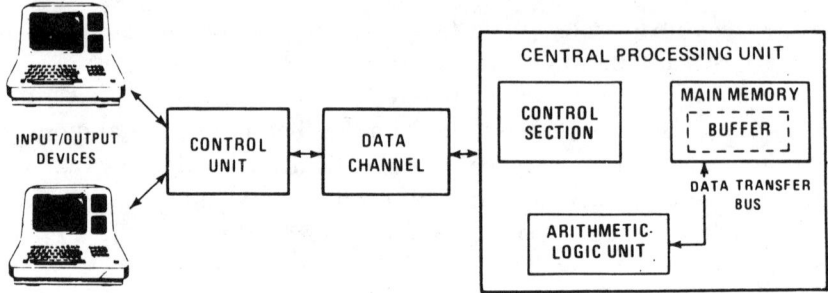

FIGURE 5. Basic Concepts of Data Entry

this discussion deal with the basic concepts of data entry and output; they do not address additional considerations raised when any of the hardware elements are geographically separated. These additional considerations are discussed under data communications.

Figure 5 illustrates the flow of data from entry to the CPU. The concepts illustrated are also valid if the data is first stored outside the CPU and then accessed for processing from secondary storage; in such a case, the control unit for the secondary-storage device locates the data for the operating system. In the data-output process, the procedures and equipment are reversed.

The interaction and timing of the input/output devices, channels, buffers, and CPU are controlled by the operating-systems hardware and software. The channels and buffers perform functions that allow the CPU to perform fast-speed data processing, which it alone is capable of performing, rather than the slower input and output operations.

Computers have built-in self-checking features that monitor the accuracy of their internal data transfer and processing. The risk that erroneous or incomplete information could be output from accurate input as a result of a hardware malfunction is extremely minor.

The electronic keyboard is the most commonly used data-input device. It can be used to enter data to cards, tape, disk, or directly to a computer via a *visual-display terminal*. A visual-display terminal may have no other capabilities (a *dumb terminal*), it may have processing capabilities (a *smart terminal*), or it may also be programmable (an *intelligent terminal*). Microcomputers are increasingly used as intelligent terminals when linked to a larger computer.

In addition to the keyboard, there are several other input devices in general use. *Magnetic-ink character readers (MICRs)* are used extensively by banks to read the characters printed at the bottom of checks. *Optical character readers* (OCRs) do not require special magnetic ink and can read a wide range of characters. OCRs can read alphanumeric characters and bar codes. They are used by a variety of organizations, from public utilities that record usage information as shown by meters onto special cards ready by OCRs, to retailers that use OCRs for sales/inventory processing.

Other input devices include *point-of-sale* (POS) *terminals, portable data-entry terminals, teleprinter terminals* and *automated-teller machines* (ATMs). These devices all transform data into electronic media.

DATA-OUTPUT DEVICES

The most commonly used device for data output in human-readable form is the printer. Printers are generally classified by whether they print a character or a line at a time, and whether the metal type strikes the paper. *Line printers* can print an entire line at a time, while *character printers* print only a character at a time. *Nonimpact printers* are the quieter and generally faster alternatives to the older *impact printers* that rely on a metal typeface striking the paper. The most common forms of printers used with smaller computers are the character-impact variety, either the dot-matrix or daisy-wheel type. A dot-matrix device prints a pattern of small dots to form a character, while a daisy-wheel printer uses a rotating wheel with a series of spokes, each containing a raised character. Line printers, commonly linked to larger computers, are faster than character printers. A recent advancement in line printers that has gained general business popularity is the *laser printer,* which uses a laser beam to form character images on the surface of a rotating drum. A toner that adheres to the images is then transferred to the paper. Laser printers can print as many as 20,000 lines per minute; most previous line printers could do no more than 2000 lines per minute.

Other output devices include *computer-output-to-microfilm* (COM) *devices,* and *voice-response systems,* such as those used by telephone companies for directory assistance.

Direct-access storage devices and visual-display terminals, including small computers, are increasing in popularity as organizations act to make information more broadly accessible. This is being further hastened by the fact that paper is bulkier, generally costlier, and deteriorates more quickly than electronic media.

Financial and operating information that formerly was stored on paper in several departments throughout an organization may now be concentrated in centrally located electronic-storage files accessed by small computers. This is an important factor to consider when evaluating the risk of (ease of making) unauthorized additions, deletions, or alterations to significant financial information.

SUMMARY OBSERVATIONS

Computers of all sizes and makes basically work similarly; differences relate to processing speed, size of primary and secondary memory, and the code (EBCDIC or ASCII) they use.

Most data and programs are stored on secondary-storage media and are only brought into the computer's main memory when needed to perform a given task. Examples of secondary storage are: magnetic disks, optical (laser) disks, and magnetic tape.

A wide variety of data-input and data-output devices are in use today. They range from the keyboard and printer to more esoteric devices, such as optical character readers, automated-teller machines, and laser printers.

Direct-access storage and visual-display terminals are increasing in popularity as organizations act to make information more broadly accessible.

Financial and operating information that was formerly stored in several departments may increasingly be concentrated in centrally located electronic-storage files.

11

SOFTWARE AND MORE SOFTWARE

Computer software is a set of instructions that tells the computer how to process, store, and retrieve data. Software is generally classified as either *systems software* or *application software*.

Systems software is the set of programs that allows the application software to process data using a computer. It does this by providing such standard functions as computer-language translation, data-communications monitoring, job instruction, input/output sequencing, data file-access management, sorting, and access control. Application software is a set of programs that performs specific tasks for end-users, for example, payroll or accounts payable.

To appreciate systems and application software, it is helpful to be familiar with the different levels of computer languages. *Machine languages* (or "first-generation" languages) are written in binary code (1s and 0s) that the computer understands. Each instruction has at least two parts, an *operation code* and an *operand*, that specify which operation is to be performed on which data element. *Assembly languages* ("second generation") are written in a symbolic code that assigns abbreviated symbols to operation codes and operands.

Although machine and assembly languages are typically unique to each type of computer, *high-level* or *procedural languages* ("third generation") are designed to be used in a wide variety of computers with minimal changes. Examples of high-level languages are BASIC, FORTRAN, APL, COBOL, PL/1, ALGOL, Pascal, and RPG. Each has a *compiler* written for each type of computer to translate the higher-level language into machine language.

Fourth-generation languages include *query languages* and *user-programming languages and tools*. Query languages allow data access with relative ease and are becoming increasingly useful to management. User-programming languages and support tools allow a user with relatively little programming background to create applications and manipulate data.

An important consideration is that less technical skill is required to write or modify programs written in third- or fourth-generation languages. Most EDP departments have very few people who can successfully alter machine-language programs, but some users with little data-processing background can easily modify fourth-generation language programs. The added risk of unauthorized change can be reduced by using librarian-management software and control procedures to record changes to programs written and maintained in the higher-level languages, whereby each change is recorded in a log or through the use of security software.

Systems software is generally written and maintained in assembly language, while application software generally uses third- or fourth-generation languages. Purchased application packages, however, are sometimes made available by the vendor exclusively in machine language to reduce the likelihood of unauthorized user changes.

OPERATING-SYSTEMS SOFTWARE

The operating system is a set of programs designed to:

Schedule the execution of jobs

Manage memory (i.e., assign programs to specific locations in main memory and free main memory when tasks are completed)

Manage input/output activities

Protect data in the event of a hardware or software breakdown (recovery management)

The heart of the operating system is the *supervisor program,* also known as the *monitor* or *executive program*. This program coordinates all functions of the operating system, including interaction with job control programs and activation of data channels. *Job-control programs* interpret the *job-control statements* that describe the job name, user name, input/output devices to be used, data files to be accessed, and the application or systems programs to be executed. The job-control statements are written in a *job-control language* (JCL) that is unique to each operating system.

The operating systems of most mainframes, minicomputers, and newer, larger-capacity microcomputers allow *multiprogramming*, in which multiple jobs can be processed together (integrated) rather than one at a time. In this way, the CPU is operating almost constantly instead of waiting for slower input/output devices.

Programs are assigned different levels of priority to achieve this integration. For example, immediate-update programs activated from terminals are generally given higher priority than delayed-update processing programs. Consequently, program interruptions will occur when programs with higher priority are activated as lower-priority jobs are running. When such an interruption occurs, the operating system stores intermediate program results while the higher-priority program is run. Operating-system software controls ensure that the intermediate storage and transfer of data are performed with no data alteration or loss.

If this storage were limited to main memory, the number of programs that could be executed concurrently would be constrained by the size of main memory. To avoid these constraints, the concept of *virtual storage* has been developed. Under virtual storage, a program is divided into pages of instructions. Only those pages actually required for processing (on the basis of storage-capacity constraints) are kept in main memory; other pages are temporarily stored externally on a direct-access storage device, in "virtual" storage.

Unlike multiprogramming, *multiprocessing* connects multiple CPUs and allows more than one program to be executed simultaneously. Different operating systems have varying degrees of activity reporting that are useful for implementing independent control procedures and facilitating management's review and analysis of reports. Additionally, most operating systems have some form of access-control capabilities, but because they are not as effective as specifically designed security software, teleprocessing monitors, and DBMS software, they are often not used for access control.

LANGUAGE TRANSLATORS

Application programs coded in higher-level languages must be translated into a machine language to be operational. *Assemblers* translate from assembly language and *compilers* translate from a third- or fourth-generation language. The process translates a *source program* into an *object program*.

Object programs cannot be run until they have been processed by *linkage-editor software*, or "link edited." A linkage editor groups together various dependent programs into an *executable module*. The effect of this process on the risk of unauthorized changes to application programs is as follows:

> An individual who has higher-level language programming skills only requires access to an application program in source code, a compiler, and a linkage editor to effect a change.
>
> An individual with object-code (machine-language) programming skills requires access to an application program in object code and a linkage editor (or only access to the executable modules) to effect a change.

Normally, the individuals with machine-language programming skills are systems programmers.

An alternative to the use of compilers and link editors for translation of third- and fourth-generation languages is a program called an *interpreter*. Rather than translating the source program and permanently saving the object code produced during a compiling run, the language translation is performed by the interpreter program as the job is executed.

Because each source-program statement is converted into machine-language code as it is needed during the processing of data, no separate translation run is performed. Thus, the opportunity to use the translation step to ensure that all program changes were authorized is lost when using interpreters. Additionally, the processing of data is generally slower with interpreters, although the program-generation process can be more efficient because the extra translation run is not needed.

Whether interpreters or compilers are used depends on the source-code language. For example, FORTRAN and COBOL are almost always compiled, APL is almost always interpreted, and BASIC has both compiled and interpreted versions. Additionally, most fourth-generation languages are interpreted rather than compiled.

FILE-ACCESS MANAGER SYSTEMS

File-access methods are software used to create, describe, and access data files. File-access methods include *file-access manager systems* (also called *flat-file systems*) and *database management systems* (DBMSs).

Let's first look at flat-file systems. Data in flat files may be accessed sequentially or directly (also known as randomly) depending on the:

Storage Medium. Files stored on magnetic tape can only be accessed sequentially, while files stored on direct-access storage devices (DASDs) can be accessed either sequentially or directly.

File-Access Method. A file can only be accessed directly if a direct-file access method is used.

File Structure. For direct access or relative location, a unique attribute (called a key) must be defined when the file is created. For example, the key of a customer name and address file might be the customer number, while the key of a general-ledger file might be the account number. Direct-file access method software often maintains an index of the physical locations of records with specific keys and uses that index to find a record.

Some file-access manager-software systems have password-access control capabilities, but these capabilities are not widely used. Instead, most organizations are moving toward security software for access control.

DATABASE-MANAGEMENT SYSTEMS

The main objective of using DBMS software and database files is to provide an efficient means of handling pieces of information needed by many different users, all of whom may require different views of the same data. Each of the different views is referred to as a logical data view. The logical data view provides the data elements required for each user's specific purpose. For example, a payroll department data-entry clerk for timesheets may require a logical data view containing employee number, payroll date, and hours worked. A service clerk for paycheck information may require a logical data view containing employee number, name, address, payroll data, gross amount, FICA, federal tax, deductions, and net amount.

The logical data view also defines the particular sequence in which the data is represented. For example, the same data may be required for two different applications, but in different orders. There may be one application requiring information by payroll date first, then department, staff level, and name; and a different application requiring information by staff level first, then payroll date, department, and name.

Finally, the logical data view describes the type of actions permitted on each data element in the view. For example, the service clerk for paycheck information may be defined in the logical view as only having the ability to read the insurance-deduction information on a paycheck. The insurance-adjustment clerk, through a different logical view, may be able to read, change, or delete the insurance-deduction information.

All data elements in a database and the physical relationships in which they are stored are referred to as the physical view of the data. The logical data view presents its view of a set of data elements on the database regardless of the physical storage. In order to access data as it is physically stored, the DBMS usually uses *pointers*. A pointer is the address of the physical location of data. Pointers allow a DBMS to locate, access, and assemble the physical-data elements included in a logical data view. For example, the logical data view containing invoice number, date, and amount may access invoice number and date from one physical location and amount from another physical location in the database.

DBMS software is used to reflect the logical relationship of the pieces of data and how they interact with application programs. Because data stored by the DBMS is independent of the application programs that use the data, either the programs or the data can be changed without disrupting the other. In a DBMS, data elements required by multiple users can be shared, thus eliminating the need to duplicate the same data in separate files.

The physical layout of data stored in database files is generally different from that in traditional flat files, which are separate files of data, with each file usually organized using a single key field. A database can be accessed in several ways because it can contain pointers to many different keys. This provides substantial flexibility for systems modifications. It may help reduce or eliminate data duplicated in separate files. Furthermore, access through a DBMS can provide an increased level of data security, because access paths may be more controllable.

This access control can be provided in two ways. First, an identification code and password system may be used to allow access to terminals, files, fields, programs, or portions of programs to any user after the proper identification code and password are entered. Second, user profiles may be used to predefine the authorized data elements (that is, the logical view) with which the user can interact. The only way to gain further access to data is to change the profile in the DBMS or to use someone else's identifying code and password.

Frequently, installation of a sophisticated database system necessitates the appointment of a *database administrator* (DBA) with responsibility for the overall design and maintenance of the database and liaison with user departments sharing the system. The DBA's responsibilities include maintenance of a *data dictionary/directory system* (often simply called a *data dictionary*). The data dictionary is a description of the data contained in the database, including the name, type, usage, field size, and source of the data, as well as the application programs authorized to use the data.

An *active data dictionary* is used by the language translator to include data format and user profiles in application programs. If a compiler or assembler is used to translate source programs into machine language, changes to the data dictionary will be reflected in the application programs when they are recompiled or reassembled. Programs that are run without recompilation or reassembly will not reflect data-dictionary changes. If an interpreter is used, changes to the data dictionary become effective immediately.

A *passive data dictionary* is maintained to provide a design tool and documentation for programmers and it is not linked to the language translator. Manual controls are therefore necessary to ensure that all changes to the data dictionary are reflected in the appropriate application programs. Although most DBMSs currently in use only have passive data-dictionary capabilities, the use of active data dictionaries is expected to increase.

A data dictionary can be an effective audit tool because it can be used to list the application programs, program functions, and users having access to various data elements. It can also be used to determine the effect of a data-element change on a financial-statement component by identifying the relationships between data elements and the programs affecting financial-statement components. An active dictionary is more useful than a passive one because it can provide assurance that the current dictionary definitions are consistent with actual application-program access to the data elements.

The access controls residing within the DBMS are only effective if access to the data is through the DBMS. For example, a systems programmer could gain access to data within a database using an *on-line editor* or a *utility* rather than a DBMS. *Security software* is therefore also needed to prevent unauthorized access to data by directly protecting the data from all access paths.

Although a database management system includes features that can be used to structure database files to reduce data redundancy and improve data independence, an organization may at times correctly choose not to use those features. The resulting files, although accessed through the DBMS, resemble flat files.

Various DBMSs have different logical structures for reflecting the relationships between the data segments. The most common such structures are *hierarchical, network,* and *relational.* These relationships affect the order and method of accessing data and generally have no effect on audit risk, although the relational structure most readily facilitates the ad hoc retrieval of information for audit or other purposes.

The DBMS does not ensure the integrity of data by providing control totals, balancing controls, edit and validation controls, or other programmed document-processing controls. Controls to ensure that data is complete, authentic, and fairly presented need to be included in application software and/or the active data dictionary.

Databases are often used for decision support systems, that may have no direct effect on the accuracy of other financial systems. For example, an organization may process all sales, purchases, and payroll transactions through a conventional flat-file system and then transfer information from the transaction-processing system files to a database system. In this example, the database system provides the tools required to support ad hoc access by managers throughout the organization to information for marketing, purchasing, hiring, and other decisions. Controls would be required to ensure that the database system cannot be used to add, delete, or alter the information obtained from the transaction processing system.

Although there certainly is a business risk in making a decision based on inaccurate information, the reliability of other financial data prepared from the transaction-processing system is not affected by errors in the database system itself.

The strengths of a DBMS relative to file-access manager software are:

Sharing of data between users to reduce redundancy and inconsistency

Controlling data access through use of identification codes, passwords, and user profiles

Allowing greater independence of data from the applications using the data, a feature that facilitates flexibility in constructing and modifying application programs

Improving data recoverability through restart and recovery software (Most file-access managers do not have these capabilities, although they can be implemented through the use of other systems software)

Potential drawbacks of a DBMS relative to file-access manager software are:

More expensive and complex hardware and software is often necessary.

A lengthy conversion process may be required to change from a conventional system to a database system.

Employees may be reluctant to adapt to the resulting changes in an information system.

Without the proper access controls, unauthorized changes to data files are sometimes easier to effect.

OTHER SYSTEMS SOFTWARE

Other commonly used systems-software programs are:

Security software
Librarian-management software
Operations-management software
On-line editors
Teleprocessing monitors
Utility programs
Communications-control software

Security Software

Security software is systems software designed to restrict access to sensitive system resources (e.g., programs and data files) to only authorized users. When installed, security software is normally the primary means of protecting data and application programs. Access is based on security profiles maintained by the software that describes the users authorized to access particular elements, such as data files, programs, and terminals. As an example, security software might use identification codes to identify authorized users of a given terminal and data file, would prevent unauthorized use of the terminal or access to the data file, and would make a record of unsuccessful attempts. The available packages vary in their methods of identifying the user, the access paths (e.g., delayed-update processing jobs, immediate update processing) they control, their response to security violations, and the maintenance of a transaction trail.

Librarian-Management Software

Librarian programs perform an important control function by maintaining the date of the most recent modification to each application program, a log of application-program changes, and two or more versions of each application program. Programmers normally work with inactive test versions rather than production versions of programs in making modifications. These modified programs should be tested and approved before they are placed in production. In addition to providing an audit trail of the program change control process, librarian software also provides the facilities to control access to production programs.

Operations-Management Software

Operations management software includes tape and disk management systems, as well as job schedulers. Its primary purpose is to improve the operating efficiency of computerized information systems, but it also provides access control. Tape- and disk-management systems can be used to ensure that the correct tape or disk is mounted for data-file processing. Job-scheduling software allows data-processing management to establish a schedule of the jobs to be run each day and the order of those jobs. The ability to make schedule changes can be limited to appropriate personnel and a listing can be produced of all such changes.

On-Line Editors

On-line editors are systems software designed to provide functions enabling applications programmers to more easily write programs, process test data by directly entering and modifying source code in an on-line environment (i.e, direct interaction with the operating system), and execute and use systems software, such as utilities. Most application programs are written this way in systems that have on-line editors. Editors vary in their ease of use, degree of risk (such as ease of gaining access to system resources), facilities to submit processing jobs, and available utility functions for maintaining program libraries (such as copying and renaming programs). Due to the flexibility and features of on-line editors a number of systems are being created that use the on-line editor as part of the production program.

Teleprocessing Monitors

Teleprocessing monitors are systems software designed to control the execution of application programs in an on-line environment. Teleprocessing monitors typically include access controls over data files and the transactions that can be executed from terminals. They handle the functions of:

- Screen display
- File access
- Restart and recovery
- Receipt of data
- Invocation of various application programs

Utility Programs

Utilities perform useful administrative functions, such as:

- Sorting records into a particular sequence
- Merging and copying files
- Printing file dumps

These administrative functions usually pose only limited major document-processing controls risk (although some have file-copying and access-control features). However, there is a special type of utility that allows a user to change executable program libraries and data files, among other things, without the creation of an easily accessible record of having done so. Although use of these utilities requires a high level of sophistication, their use should be carefully controlled.

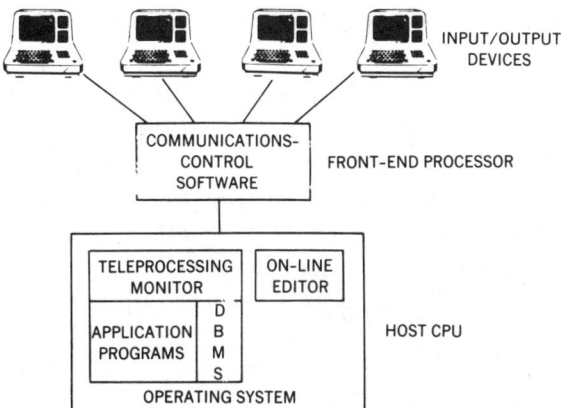

FIGURE 6. Relationship of Communications-Control Software to Other Software

Communications-Control Software

Communications-control software is systems software designed to manage information flow between users at various terminals and host computers. The relationship between communications software and other software is illustrated in Figure 6.

Generally, communications-control software is resident in a front-end processor, as depicted. In some systems, however, the communications-control software may be resident in the host CPU.

Software such as teleprocessing monitors, DBMS, and on-line editors use only a logical address of the various input/output devices; the physical locations of these devices within the network structure are invisible to them. Communications-control software provides this link by defining the relationship between the logical addresses and the physical devices. The communications-control software generally contains tables of source/destination device identification codes. That is, the association of a physical-terminal address and a logical-terminal name are defined in these tables. There is the potential for someone to circumvent the access-control features of other software by changing the information contained in these tables.

For example, let's say the access tables within a teleprocessing monitor were designed to allow only the payroll department's terminal (logical address) to enter payroll transactions and the accounts-payable department's terminal (logical address) to enter accounts-payable transactions. In this situation, it is possible that someone could modify the logical/physical relationship of these terminals within the table of communications-control software to enable payroll transactions, for example, to be entered from the accounts-payable department. However, the risk of this occurring is fairly low because it takes a knowledgeable systems programmer to effect such a change. Also, this risk is only present if an organization is using terminal identification (as opposed to passwords or other user-supplied information) as an access control.

APPLICATION SOFTWARE

Application (or user) software consists of programs written to perform specific tasks for users. These programs (such as general ledger, payroll, accounts receivable, and accounts payable) can be developed in-house or purchased from software vendors.

Software packages can be purchased in either source or object code. Vendors prefer to supply only the object-code versions because they are more difficult to modify. Many vendors offer object-code versions that have "user exits," which allow the purchaser to tailor certain parts of the programs to specific needs.

Application software frequently needs to be altered to meet changing user needs. For this reason, applications are often written and maintained in languages that facilitate changes. It is, however, important to control the environment in which these changes are made to ensure that only authorized changes are made to production programs.

SUMMARY OBSERVATIONS

The most powerful tools for controlling access to programs and data and detecting authorized changes to programs and data are computer software. These tools have become especially important since computerized information systems have moved out of carefully segregated computer facilities. Access control can no longer be provided solely by controlling physical access to the computer facilities.

Although access controls can be included in several different types of systems software, specially designed security software is usually the best means of protecting data and application programs.

Alteration of programs maintained only in machine language requires more technical skill than alteration of those programs in third- or fourth-generation language, but does not require access to a compiler for the change to be effective.

Librarian-management software can keep a record (log) of changes to application programs.

A potential control safeguard is lost when an interpreter is used because the separate step of compiling from source code to object code is no longer necessary when a program is changed.

Balancing controls normally reside within application software, but are more difficult to design for database files.

A DBMS is frequently used for decision-support systems that may have no direct effect on the accuracy of the financial statements because the computerized processing of transactions is separate from the DBMS used for decision support.

Some fourth-generation languages only allow the user to read data without altering it, although others allow the alteration of data.

Certain general-use utility programs allow program or data changes without creating an easily accessible record of the data changed.

12

DATA COMMUNICATIONS

Data communications is an increasing part of everyday business life. Unfortunately, unless sensible precautions are taken, communications capability increases vulnerability to:

Unauthorized access to programs, data files, and data-processing equipment (possibly resulting in information theft, erroneous or fraudulent transactions, or vandalism)

Errors during transmission (possibly causing lost, distorted, or duplicated information)

It is important to understand the concepts of data communications as an aid in identifying the business implications of data communications.

The purpose of *data communications* is to transfer data between computers, external devices, or terminals. To accomplish this movement of data, hardware and software components use a combination of computer and telecommunications technology. (*Telecommunications* is the technology used to establish a communications link between two or more locations.)

Data communications is becoming a feature of more and more computer systems, regardless of their system structure. For example, distributed data processing depends on the use of data-communications facilities to function. Because both centralized and decentralized systems frequently use input and output devices, including small com-

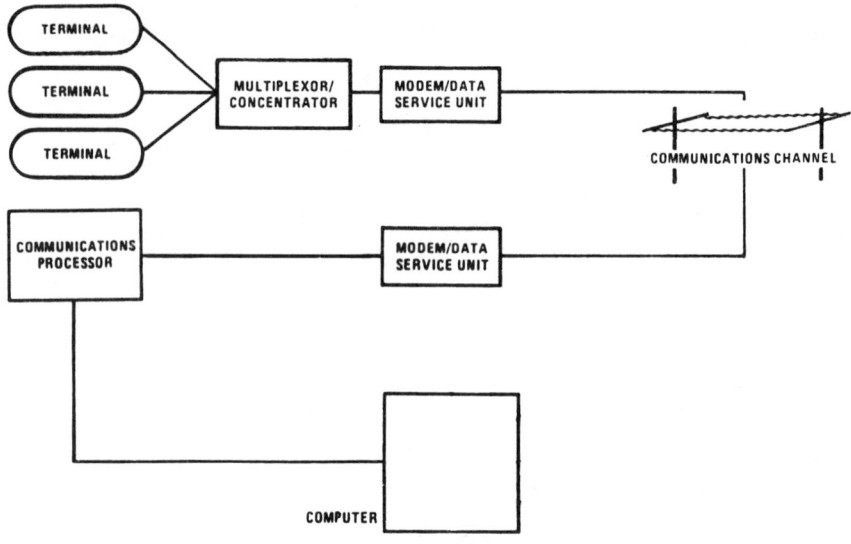

FIGURE 7. Line Multiplexors

puters positioned at locations remote from the large computer, both use data-communications facilities to connect these remote devices to the computer. Data communications can be used to operate either in an immediate-update or a delayed-update processing mode.

COMMUNICATIONS HARDWARE

A typical data-communications system (see Figure 7) consists of the following hardware: terminals, *line multiplexors* or *concentrators*, *modulator-demodulator devices* (*modems*) or *data-service units*, *communications channels, communications processors*, and one or more computers (one of which may be known as the *host*). Each of these devices, with the exception of terminals and computers, will be discussed.

Line Multiplexors

Line multiplexors are devices that transform relatively low-speed data from a number of sources, such as terminals, to a higher-speed single stream of data for transmission on a single communications channel. Their primary function is to permit a number of terminals to concurrently share a single line; by doing this, multiplexors maximize the efficient use of communications links in a network. The same function is often performed by similar devices called concentrators, which are programmable and more flexible, but also more expensive.

Modem

Telephone facilities have been the major carrier of data because of their widespread availability and their capability to access virtually every point in the country. Telephone facilities, however, were designed to enhance voice communications and some special apparatus and techniques must be used to transmit data over these channels. A modem is the most basic of these and is used to transform the data from digital-pulse form to continuous-wave (audible) form at the transmitting location and back to digital pulse at the receiving location. Simply stated, a modem acts as a translator between the computer, which speaks one language (digital or "pulse"), and the telecommunications channel, which speaks another (analog or "wave").

As an alternative to using the "voice" channels, *digital-transmission facilities* have come into use in recent years. Facilities of this type transmit data in bit streams directly, without first converting them to an analog format. Direct connection to a digital-transmission facility requires a digital interface, called a data-service unit, between the user's equipment and the service. These interfaces replace modems and are much less complex than modems. The primary advantage of digital transmission (versus analog) is that it is less sensitive to error-causing electrical interference during transmission. As a result, digital transmission yields overall error-rate performance superior to that of analog transmission. A disadvantage is that digital services are not currently available in many areas.

Communications Channels

Communications channels differ from the data channels described in the hardware chapter. Data channel refers to the equipment and cable that interconnect computers to peripheral devices (e.g., auxiliary storage). They act as a governor of the flow of information between the computer and the peripheral devices to compensate for the differences in the speed with which the computer and peripheral devices move information. Communications channels serve only as a communications medium. Communications channels are classified according to the volume of data they are capable of transporting. *Narrowband* (also known as baseband), *voiceband,* and *broadband* channels, respectively, carry increasing volumes of data. Small coaxial cables and telegraph lines are examples of narrowband channels, while telephone lines are a good example of a voiceband channel. Examples of broadband channels include: larger coaxial cables, microwave circuits, and communications-satellite channels.

At present, the telephone line is the most commonly used medium for communicating data. Telephone lines can be used either on a dial-up, packet-switched, or private (leased-line) basis. These methods as well as other methods of communicating data are discussed later in this section.

Communications Processors

Between the modem and the computer, there is usually a device called a communications processor, normally a minicomputer dedicated solely to managing data communications. By performing this function, communications processors relieve the main computer of much of the processing and memory utilization ("overhead") involved in message handling and network control.

TRANSMISSION, CIRCUITS, AND COMMUNICATIONS SOFTWARE

Transmission

The two basic modes of transmitting data are *synchronous* and *asynchronous*. In the latter mode, also known as start-stop transmission, each character sent over the line is preceded and followed by start and stop control elements, respectively. This mode is appropriate for slower transmission that may come at irregular intervals; for example, when input from an electronic-keyboard terminal.

Synchronous mode accommodates faster transmission. Data is transmitted in an even stream with the transmitter and receiver synchronized so that the start-stop elements are not needed.

Circuits

There are three basic types of transmission circuits: *simplex, half duplex,* and *duplex*. A simplex circuit permits data to flow in only one direction. A half-duplex circuit permits data flow in either direction, but only one direction at a time. Duplex circuits allow data transmission in both directions simultaneously.

Half-duplex and duplex circuits are the most commonly used. Duplex circuits are the faster of the two since they avoid the delays that occur in half-duplex circuits each time the direction of transmission is changed. Simplex circuits are seldom used because a terminal connected to this type of circuit is either a send-only or a receive-only device. A return path would generally be needed to send acknowledgment, control, or error signals.

Communications Software

Even in its most primitive form, teleprocessing software is complex. In primitive systems, all teleprocessing software is processed in the host computer. In a more contemporary system, where the communications processor is a computer itself, much of the software for data-communications functions is resident in that computer. Further sophistication comes into play when the remote-control unit is also a computer (e.g., a concentrator handling the tasks related to the terminal devices connected to it).

In a typical data-communications environment, many terminals are being used concurrently for data retrieval or entry of transactions. Software programs are required to receive these messages, locate the proper application program that is being addressed, load that program into memory, and pass the message to that program for processing. On completion of processing, data-communications software is required to send the response back to the requester.

Additionally, data-communications software programs are required to handle any errors that might be included in the transactions being received. Sophisticated systems have substantial error-recovery capabilities. Simple systems usually are only capable of rejecting the transaction and notifying the user at the terminal from which it was sent.

Teleprocessing software should have the capability to keep a log of transactions and a database or file of records that have been updated by the transactions. The log can be used for restart and recovery in the event of a computer malfunction.

Additionally, data-communications software must manage buffer pools. *Buffers* are the area of computer storage set aside as staging areas to hold transactions and messages pending processing. As is by now apparent to you, the software is very sophisticated. In a more elaborate environment, data communications becomes more complicated because more hardware elements are involved and more software is in use. The CPU in this situation would still contain data-communications software (quite likely more than in a simple system), and the front-end processor and the concentrator would also contain data-communications software.

In the data-communications area, a principal concern to management is the risk of unauthorized access to, or manipulation of, data. Usually, communications protocols, which ensure accurate transmission of data, are part of each communication network. As a result, message error generally is not an area that presents significant concern. Features of communications protocols will be discussed later in this chapter.

A series of messages must be exchanged between the transmitter and the receiver of a message whenever data is transmitted. This series of messages is designed to:

Ensure that the data is sent to the proper destination

Detect and correct transmission errors

Control the sequence of messages sent and received

Each transmission software has its own set of rules or *protocol* for performing these functions. The most commonly used protocols are SDLC (Synchronous-Data Link Control), Bisync (Binary Synchronous), and TTY (Teletype). Protocols vary in the amount of error checking that is performed and the methods used for determining destinations and sequences of messages.

An example of a more sophisticated protocol is *message authentication*. This technique uses advanced mathematical formulas to calculate a self-checking code based on the data being sent. When the data is received, the code is recalculated and the results of the two calculations are compared. Any variation indicates that a transmission error has occurred and appropriate steps are taken to correct it.

A technique for guarding against unauthorized access to data being transmitted is known as *encryption* or enciphering. This may be done by using a program prior to transmission that converts or encrypts the data to a format that cannot be understood without knowledge of the encryption formula and key. The code cannot be read until it is decrypted at the destination point. Different encryption programs have differing degrees of sophistication. In addition to software programs, hardware devices that encrypt and decrypt data are also available.

NETWORKS AND SERVICE ORGANIZATIONS

Earlier, it was pointed out that organizations using data-communications technology are potentially vulnerable to unauthorized access and errors occurring during message transmission. This section discusses the major types of data-communications networks available and the different levels of exposure associated with each level.

Data-communications networks are vehicles that provide the connections necessary to allow data transfer between system components that need to communicate (such as CPUs and terminals). Network facilities can be categorized into four groups:

Private networks
Public-switched networks
Value-added networks
Local-area networks

The first three groups, covered in this section, are wide-area network facilities. These networks can cover unlimited distances and for transmission use data-communications facilities, such as telephone lines, microwave channels, or communications-satellite channels. Local-area networks (LANs), on the other hand, transmit data over coaxial cable, fiber-optics cable, or similar media, and are limited in the distance they can cover (typically, they do not extend more than a mile or so).

Private Networks

Private networks, also called *leased* or *dedicated lines,* are transmission facilities obtained typically from a common carrier for dedicated use by the lessee organization. Common carriers are organizations authorized to provide transmission services.

In a private network, the organization's computerized system is directly connected to the common carrier for data transmission. No dial-up to access the common carrier's facilities is necessary. In addition to telephone lines, microwave and satellite facilities are often used.

The advantage of a private network is that the connection is always available and data can be transferred at any time with no wait to establish a connection. This contrasts with the use of a switched (dial-up) network, where a connection must be established each time data transfer is required, and competition for use of the network facilities may make it impossible to establish a connection when it is needed.

Two major advantages of private networks over public lines are that private networks generally allow for a higher rate of data transmission, and the user can usually specify the characteristics of the line to help ensure the quality of transmission, which reduces message errors and thereby increases efficiency. However, private networks may be more expensive, especially if usage is low.

Since the network connection is not made by use of a dial-up facility, it is generally more difficult for outsiders to gain unauthorized access to a private network than to a public-switched network. Vulnerability to eavesdropping by means of a wiretap, on the other hand, is greater where leased/dedicated lines are involved because the lines through which transmissions are sent are fixed and usually clearly identified in the organization's switching center. This contrasts with a public-switched or dial-up network, where lines used for transmission will vary.

Data communication using microwave- or satellite-transmission technologies is especially vulnerable to eavesdropping. Although the possibility of eavesdropping generally will not present an audit risk, the business risks can be considerable. For this reason, management should consider the use of data-encryption techniques in instances where secret information is transmitted over any data-communications network.

Public-Switched Networks

Public-switched networks use regular public-telephone communications facilities to transfer data. When switched networks are used, a dial-up connection must be established each time a data transmission session is required between the two endpoints.

A switched network is often the best choice economically if two locations need to exchange data only infrequently and they can afford to wait when no connection is available. Sometimes an attempt to obtain a connection results in a busy signal, either because the endpoint is already connected to another location or because the network circuits are overloaded.

Another disadvantage of a switched network, in contrast to a private link, is that data-transmission quality may vary enormously. Sometimes data transmission may proceed with few or no data errors; at other times, a large number of transmission errors may occur. One reason for the variability of errors on the public networks is their method of routing; a call between the same two endpoints may travel over different routes at different times, and some routes may include equipment which is more error-prone than that on other routes. Also, some types of transmission facilities are sensitive to disturbances, such as weather (for example, thunderstorms), that can cause data errors during transmission. Fortunately, very effective hardware and software techniques are generally employed to detect and correct line errors, thereby enhancing network reliability.

Public-switched networks provide the least amount of protection against unauthorized access of any of the network types. Anyone can call the computer if they have a terminal or microcomputer equipped with the appropriate communications facilities and knowledge of the telephone number of a computer system having "auto-answer" dial-in facilities (i.e., no manual-operator intervention is required to connect the call).

Depending on the privileges assigned to the dial-in port that the unauthorized user has accessed, that individual may gain access to system-level and/or application-level functions. Further, microcomputers can be programmed to attempt to enter a password-protected system by repeatedly calling the computer and trying a different password combination each time. This type of "brute force" attack will be successful unless security software is used to slow down the attack; for example, software could disconnect the dialer after three or so unsuccessful attempts.

Value-Added Networks

Value-added networks (VANs) are public facilities, shared just as the telephone networks are shared, but they provide for data transmission only. The term "value-added network" is used because the organizations that operate networks of this type obtain their basic transmission facilities from other organizations, add a value (e.g., by providing the switching computers that tie the network together), and then resell the facilities to their customers. Automatic error detection and correction for data transmitted over the network facilities is another value-added service.

There are two classes of VANs. One class uses *packet-switching* techniques to transmit data, the other uses *circuit-switching* techniques. In a packet-switched network (the most prevalent type of VAN), organizations send data over telephone facilities on a dial-up basis to a local installation of the VAN. The VAN breaks up the data into fixed-length packets and transmits the packets at high speed to its installation nearest the sending organization's receiving station. The data is reassembled and then transmitted, generally over a leased line, to its destination.

Because packets from different messages can be interspersed and short messages, such as transactions, need not wait for the completion of long messages, such as jobs or files, segmenting messages into packets allows efficient use of the network links. The network ensures that the data are delivered to the correct endpoint and that any transmission errors or problems in the network are corrected or bypassed. The correct delivery of the data, end to end, is the responsibility of the network supplier.

Circuit-switched VANs are very much like the public-switched networks; however, these networks are used only for data. Unlike the packet-switched networks, the circuit-switched networks provide a dedicated link for the duration of the connection, without sharing among the different users of the network. When data transfer is complete, one of the endpoints involved must break the connection by notifying the VAN.

Packet-switched and circuit-switched VANs have somewhat different capabilities and somewhat different advantages. Packet switching is a very efficient and often low-cost way to send small amounts of data (e.g., transactions and responses) among large numbers of endpoints, especially if the pattern of connections among the endpoints changes often and is difficult to predict.

Circuit switching, in contrast, can be costly when used to send transactions and responses unless these occur continuously and, in effect, need a dedicated circuit. (In that case, a private network is usually a better choice.) It takes time to establish a circuit and the VAN supplier usually charges a fee for each time a circuit is established and broken. The supplier also usually charges for the time during which the circuit remains in operation, so that keeping a circuit in place when no data is being transmitted can be expensive. On the other hand, circuit switching is well suited to the transfer of files, jobs, or other relatively high-volume data streams because the cost of establishing a circuit is generally worthwhile for each transmission.

LOCAL-AREA NETWORKS

What about linking small computers together? For example, microcomputer users working in the same office or department often need to exchange information, such as budget or marketing statistics; small computer users also may require the occasional use of expensive peripheral equipment, such as letter-quality printers, graphic plotters, and hard disks. As a result, several hardware and software vendors have developed local-area networks (LANs).

Typically, LANs exist outside of the control of the data-processing function. Often LANs serve only a limited number of users, such as one department. Due to their increasing popularity, it is important to understand LAN environments and related security issues.

Availability of Data

Currently, LANs that are available have been designed specifically to facilitate the transfer of data between small computers. As a result, the issue of availability of data is not nearly as complex in a LAN environment as that posed by linking small computers to mainframes because, from the start, all machines to be networked "speak the same language" (ASCII). There are, however, two issues in this area that must be addressed when considering a LAN for your organization.

The first issue is compatibility, and it is extremely important. Some LANs require that all computers connected to the network must be compatible; most LANs, in fact, will support only one particular computer brand, or a very limited number of different brands. Although there are LANs that will support the connection of several different brands of small computers to the network at the same time, movement of data between incompatible machines is difficult and time-consuming. Likewise, the use of several different brands of electronic spreadsheets, word-processing packages, and so forth will also make the transfer of data between small computers connected to a LAN difficult.

LANs can be connected to mainframe computers or other LANs through the use of a gateway facility (hardware and software that link a LAN to a mainframe or another LAN). The compatibility issues discussed previously and, more importantly, the availability-of-data issues that arise when small computers are linked to mainframes must also be addressed if you are considering connecting a LAN with another network.

Most of the LANs currently available are purchased as "kits" (hardware and software are generally provided by a single vendor). In addition to a "wire" that physically connects the machines, components of a LAN typically consist of the following:

Communication boards that are inserted in one of the expansion slots of the microcomputers, thereby enabling the small computers to be connected to the network

Network server and software that control network communications and data storage (the network server is usually a microcomputer dedicated to this purpose)

Large-capacity hard disk for data storage

Installing and connecting these devices are complex activities and should be performed by the vendor or other personnel possessing the necessary data-processing experience and training. Also, do not overlook the importance of day-to-day maintenance and monitoring of the LAN; these activities will require greater training and expertise than those required to use a microcomputer in a standalone environment. Generally, a professional from your data-processing department should provide this technical assistance.

Microcomputer users typically store their programs and data on the LAN's hard disk. Often, application-software packages are stored on the hard disk and shared among users. Sharing of application-software programs in such circumstances presents potential violations of licensing and copyright agreements. Check with each particular software vendor before storing application software on your network's hard disk.

The size and capacity of the network's hard disk is another important operational consideration. User needs, network expansion, and possible connection to the mainframe should be addressed prior to deciding on the capacity of the network's hard disk.

Finally, backup and recovery is a critical issue. Using a hard disk in a network is very much like using a hard disk in a standalone application. Basically, users should ensure that important data files are backed up as frequently as they would be if the data had been stored on floppy disks. Because LANs typically involve multiple users and large volumes of data, backup is probably best done by a designated employee who backs up all data stored on the network's hard disk periodically (e.g., daily). Backup can be accomplished with a cassette tape or another hard disk.

Data security becomes an issue in a LAN environment when users store their data files (including data downloaded from the mainframe)

on the network's shared hard disk. Most LANs have some data-security measures built into the networking software but, unfortunately, these measures are not nearly as sophisticated or well-developed as those available in the mainframe environment. In fact, data-security measures available in the LAN environment often offer little more protection than those available when microcomputers are used as standalone machines. As a result, highly sensitive data should generally not be stored on a LAN's hard disk.

Although LAN security is limited, you should, nonetheless, use whatever security measures are available for your LAN and inquire about data security when purchasing a LAN. Limited password protection and logging facilities are available for some LANs. Further, LAN vendors are beginning to recognize the importance of data security in a LAN environment and are developing measures to make LAN-resident data more secure.

There are three basic topologies employed in LANs: ring, bus, and star. As you can well imagine, the physical arrangement of each type of configuration can best be described by its name.

Ring

Ring networks consist of small computers arranged in a circle or loop. Each computer or user station is dependent on the previous stations in the network for receiving or transmitting data. As data is transmitted, it is passed through each station in the network. Each computer receives the data and must then determine whether or not that data was intended for that particular address. An address is the means by which the network identifies unique stations (micros or printers) within the physical layout of each configuration. In other words, an address is the place where each computer "lives." Because of the way in which data is transmitted within the ring topology, the entire network will fail if one of the stations fails. (See Figure 8.)

Bus

In the bus configuration, computers are attached to a line that is strung around the area to be networked. This type of arrangement makes it relatively easy to add stations to the network by adding to the line. An

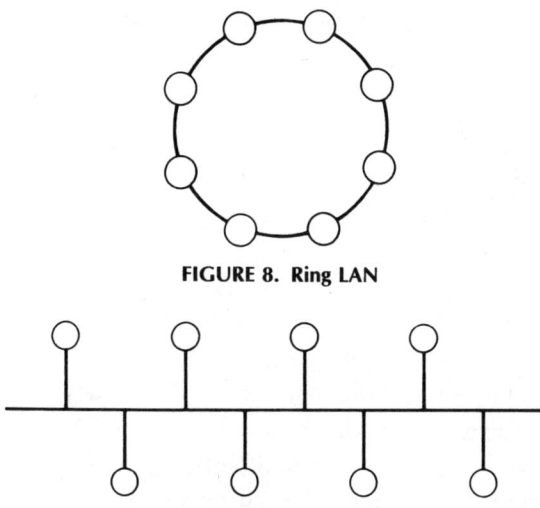

FIGURE 8. Ring LAN

FIGURE 9. Bus LAN

important feature of this type of network is that the network will continue to function should one or more computer stations fail. (See Figure 9.)

Star

Star networks contain a number of lines extending from a central computer to individual terminals or computers. The weakness of the star topology is the dependence on the central computer. If it should fail, all transmissions will cease and the network will be nonoperational. On the other hand, the failure of one computer on a point of the star will not affect the rest of the network. (See Figure 10.)

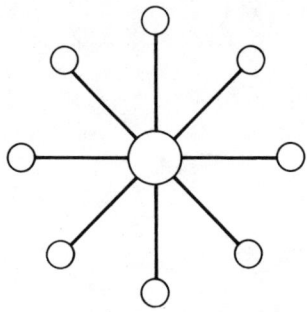

FIGURE 10. Star LAN

SUMMARY OBSERVATIONS

Once communications capabilities become part of an organization's computerized information system, that system becomes vulnerable to the risks of unauthorized access and errors in message transmission.

The degree of vulnerability to unauthorized access and the likelihood of occurrence of message error differ with the type of communications network in use.

Management of every organization employing data-communications networks must consider the adequacy of their access controls; data-encryption and authentication techniques; and hardware, software and other procedures in place to identify and correct errors that may occur during message transmission.

Data-security measures currently available in many local-area networks are relatively unsophisticated and often do not offer adequate protection for highly sensitive data.

APPENDIX

MICROCOMPUTER AND DATA SECURITY SURVEY AND RESULTS

Questionnaires covering the use, management, and control of microcomputers were mailed to representatives of organizations selected primarily from the membership lists of the National Association of Accountants, the sponsor of the research study. The organizations selected covered a cross-section of American business—geographically dispersed, varying in size, and representing different lines of business; the selection included both organizations that are sophisticated users of micros (often having more than 100 units) and organizations that have only a few microcomputers. The selection process was subjective and not designed to provide a basis for statistical conclusions.

The initial questionnaire was mailed to approximately 230 individuals at 100 organizations in 1984; an updated questionnaire was subsequently obtained from the same individuals who had responded to the earlier survey. Whenever possible, the corporate-accounting officer, data-processing officer, and internal auditor of each selected organization were included in the survey. This approach provided different perspectives, especially in response to the evaluation question on the importance of controls. Not all organizations surveyed had data-processing officers or internal auditors.

Responses to the 1984 survey were received from 138 individuals

(60 percent response rate) representing 83 organizations (83 percent response rate). The same individuals who responded to the 1984 survey were surveyed again for the 1986 survey. The response rate in 1986 was 50 percent representing 77 organizations (61 percent of the organizations).

MICROCOMPUTER/DATA SECURITY SURVEY

	1986 Update			1984 Survey		
	Percentages for Companies Responding That Have:		Percentages for All Companies Responding to This Survey	Percentages for Companies Responding That Have:		Percentages for All Companies Responding to This Survey
Question	Less Than 25 Micro-computers	25 or More Micro-computers		Less Than 25 Micro-computers	25 or More Micro-computers	
1. In what applications are microcomputers being used in your company?						
Stand-alone accounting (consolidation, general ledger, accounts receivable, etc.)	56	47	49	45	60	52
Online access (read only) to accounting and other corporate records	13	55	45	10	45	28
Online date entry to accounting and other corporate records	25	24	24	8	25	18
Engineering/research & development accounting and other corporate records	13	29	25	18	30	24
Mailing lists	31	61	54	23	53	36
Electronic mail	19	51	43	10	40	25
Budgeting/forecasting	81	98	94	65	95	81
Word processing	94	88	90	55	80	69
Cash management	19	51	43	20	33	27
Telex	0	20	15	10	8	10
Timesharing	13	37	31	20	38	28
Process control	13	18	16	5	15	10

Question	1986 Update			1984 Survey		
	Percentages for Companies Responding That Have:		Percentages for All Companies Responding to This Survey	Percentages for Companies Responding That Have:		Percentages for All Companies Responding to This Survey
	Less Than 25 Micro-computers	25 or More Micro-computers		Less Than 25 Micro-computers	25 or More Micro-computers	
Computer Assisted Manufacturing	6	14	12	3	15	9
Sales and marketing statistics and modeling	50	76	70	48	58	51
Other	25	41	37	28	30	29
2. Has your company established management policies covering the use of microcomputers?						
Yes	63	71	69	50	63	57
No	37	29	31	50	37	43
If yes, were those policies established by those officials in your organization charged with the responsibility of establishing and monitoring management policies covering "traditional EDP environments" (that is, mainframe installations, etc.)? (*Note:* Percentages based on number of organizations answering yes to first part of this question.)						
Yes	100	92	93	90	84	87
No	0	8	7	10	16	13

	Yes/No					
And if yes, does your company provide microcomputer users with a manual or other documentation which sets forth management policies with respect to microcomputers? (*Note*: Percentages based on number of organizations answering yes to the first part of the question.)						
Yes	25	35	33	30	56	45
No	75	65	67	70	44	55
And if yes, does this manual provide guidance in the area of controls? (*Note*: Percentages based on number of organizations answering yes to the first part of the question.)						
Yes	100	83	86	30	44	38
No	0	17	14	70	56	62
3. Has your company established a policy(ies) covering the acquisition of microcomputers and microcomputer software?						
Yes	81	92	90	78	88	83
No	19	8	10	22	12	17
If yes, under what departments or groups does the responsibility for carrying out this policy(ies) fall? (*Note*: Percentages based on number of organizations answering yes to the first part of the question.)						

	1986 Update			1984 Survey		
	Percentages for Companies Responding That Have:		Percentages for All Companies Responding to This Survey	Percentages for Companies Responding That Have:		Percentages for All Companies Responding to This Survey
Question	Less Than 25 Micro-computers	25 or More Micro-computers		Less Than 25 Micro-computers	25 or More Micro-computers	
Data processing	77	85	83	61	80	71
Accounting/controller	15	15	15	29	11	20
Treasury	8	0	2	3	0	1
Other	15	21	20	23	20	22
And if yes, does this policy(ies) require standardization of microcomputers and software to ensure compatibility of applications and software? (*Note:* Percentages based on number of organizations answering yes to the first part of the question.)						
Yes	85	89	88	71	80	75
No	15	11	12	29	20	25
4. Does your company provide training to microcomputer users?						
Yes	100	98	99	73	83	78
No	0	2	1	27	17	22
If yes, what types of training are used? (*Note:* Percentages based on number of organizations answering yes to the first part of the question.)						

Internal classes	44	84	74	38	88	63
External classes	63	50	53	34	33	35
Instructional materials and tutorials purchased from third parties	63	66	65	48	72	62
Instruction by experienced users within the company	50	84	76	79	72	75
Other	6	18	15	3	12	8
5. Are microcomputers considered in data processing system plans (including mainframe/minicomputer short-range and long-range plans)?						
Yes	81	84	84	63	85	73
No	19	16	16	37	15	27
6. Does your company have a microcomputer technical group which assists users with problems?						
Yes	56	90	82	45	70	59
No	44	10	18	55	30	41
If yes, what is the background of the member(s) of this group? (*Note:* Percentages based on number of organizations answering yes to first part of this question.)						
Accounting	0	20	16	17	14	14
Other	22	28	27	17	21	18
EDP	89	96	95	94	96	96
If no, does your company have an arrangement with an outside vendor, consultant, etc., to provide						

	1986 Update			1984 Survey		
	Percentages for Companies Responding That Have:		Percentages for All Companies Responding to This Survey	Percentages for Companies Responding That Have:		Percentages for All Companies Responding to This Survey
Question	Less Than 25 Micro-computers	25 or More Micro-computers		Less Than 25 Micro-computers	25 or More Micro-computers	
assistance to users? (*Note:* Percentages based on number of organizations answering no to first part of this question.)						
Yes	57	100	75	31	42	35
No	43	0	25	69	58	65
7. Which of the following are used in your company to ensure the reliability of purchased microcomputer software?						
Extensive testing by EDP department or microcomputer control group	44	63	58	33	58	47
Extensive testing by individual user	38	33	34	33	33	31
Evaluation of other users	44	39	40	33	38	36
Evaluation of microcomputer periodicals	19	57	48	20	40	30
Purchase only popular packages which have widespread acceptance and use	44	78	70	60	60	59
8. Do users develop their own software?						

Yes	13	59	48	30	65	49
No	87	41	52	70	35	51

If yes, is there a requirement that software be tested by an authorized individual? (*Note:* Percentages based on number of organizations answering yes to first part of this question.)

Yes	0	13	13	17	42	32
No	100	87	87	83	58	68

And if yes, is there a requirement that such software be documented in accordance with established standards? (*Note:* Percentages based on number of organizations answering yes to first part of this question.)

Yes	0	27	25	25	38	32
No	100	73	75	75	62	68

9. How is access to microcomputers, software, and applications controlled?

Only authorized personnel are allowed to use particular machines	75	47	54	65	48	55
Locked rooms	38	41	40	25	33	29
Machine on/off switch is locked	0	10	7	5	7	6
Program and data diskettes are physically secured	56	80	75	55	58	58
Communications facilities are locked when in an inoperative state	0	10	7	0	15	7

	1986 Update			1984 Survey		
	Percentages for Companies Responding That Have:		Percentages for All Companies Responding to This Survey	Percentages for Companies Responding That Have:		Percentages for All Companies Responding to This Survey
Question	Less Than 25 Micro-computers	25 or More Micro-computers		Less Than 25 Micro-computers	25 or More Micro-computers	
Manual and automated computer logs are required and monitored	13	14	13	13	5	8
Password protection at the entry level	31	49	45	25	35	30
Multi-level passwords	6	20	16	8	15	11
Automatic call-back checks	0	8	6	5	3	4
Other	0	4	3	3	8	6
10. Which of the following are used to ensure backup of your microcomputers and microcomputer software?						
Backup copies of all program disks are maintained in a central location away from all microcomputers.	44	24	28	35	23	28
Backup copies of all programs are stored in a protected area (fireproof, etc.)	31	20	22	20	20	22
Backup copies of all program disks are maintained in the jacket provided with the program manual	38	51	48	33	28	29

Users are instructed to maintain backup copies of data files at regular intervals	69	100	93	65	83	75
Backup copies of data diskettes are given to user's supervisor at the end of the work day	0	2	1	0	8	4
Arrangements made with computer vendor to supply microcomputers in the event company-owned microcomputers need repair or in the event of a disaster	6	22	18	8	18	12
Policy established within the company to replace microcomputers which are in need of repair with company-owned microcomputers based on priority of users needs	6	18	15	10	20	15
Other	13	10	10	5	8	7

11. Which of the following are used to ensure the accuracy and security of data and software during processing (microcomputers in both a stand-alone and communications mode)?

Input (batch) controls	31	18	21	25	30	27
Read-but-not-write protection	6	24	19	13	38	25
Run-to-run controls	19	4	7	10	10	10
Compiled program code	0	12	9	3	8	5
Output controls	13	18	16	13	23	17
Encryption	6	8	7	0	5	2

	1986 Update			1984 Survey			
	Percentages for Companies Responding That Have:		Percentages for All Companies Responding to This Survey	Percentages for Companies Responding That Have:		Percentages for All Companies Responding to This Survey	
Question	Less Than 25 Micro-computers	25 or More Micro-computers		Less Than 25 Micro-computers	25 or More Micro-computers		
Data verification by user	56	76	72	63	73	66	
Control of changes in programs and data	31	14	18	23	13	17	
Other	0	12	9	3	8	7	

12. Regardless of the situation and circumstances at your particular company, please rank all of the following controls as they apply to microcomputer/communications environments (1—very important, 2—of moderate importance, and 3—not important or practical). (*Note:* Percentages based on total number of questionnaires returned.)

	Rank 1	Rank 2	Rank 3	Rank 1	Rank 2	Rank 3
Segregation of duties	37	24	39	26	28	46
Audit trail	64	22	13	56	28	16
Acquisition and software development policies	57	33	10	54	34	12
Backup and recovery	64	30	6	69	24	7
Documentation	58	36	6	53	40	7
Physical controls such as locks	23	35	42	20	42	38
Multi-level passwords	19	36	45	17	36	47
Input (batch) controls	29	39	32	26	33	41
Run-to-run controls	22	46	32	19	39	42

Output controls	23	47	30	23	48	29	
Read-but-not-write protection	24	41	35	24	46	30	
Compiled program code	15	42	43	13	43	44	
Encryption	5	27	68	3	27	70	
Automatic call-back checks	20	33	47	10	27	63	
Control of changes in programs and data	50	27	23	44	29	27	
Computer logs	17	37	46	20	36	44	

13. Do the microcomputers in your company communicate with other computers?

Yes	69	90	85	40	83	61
No	31	10	15	60	17	39

14. With which of the following do your microcomputers communicate? (*Note:* Percentages based on number of organizations answering yes to question 13.)

Other microcomputers within the company	18	61	53	25	58	49
Minicomputers or mainframes within the company	73	91	88	50	91	76
Word processing equipment within the company	9	48	40	6	48	35
Computers external to the company (through external time sharing network)	36	80	72	44	64	57
Other	0	7	5	0	3	2

15. What type of transmission media is used in connecting your microcomputers with other

	1986 Update			1984 Survey		
	Percentages for Companies Responding That Have:		Percentages for All Companies Responding to This Survey	Percentages for Companies Responding That Have:		Percentages for All Companies Responding to This Survey
Question	Less Than 25 Micro-computers	25 or More Micro-computers		Less Than 25 Micro-computers	25 or More Micro-computers	
computers? *(Note:* Percentages based on number of organizations answering yes to question 13.)						
Modem	91	98	96	94	94	94
Twisted pair wire	9	24	21	0	30	20
Coaxial cable	27	74	65	19	58	43
Fiber optic cable	0	4	4	0	0	0
Other	0	0	0	0	0	2
16. For which of the following are communications used in your company? *(Note:* Percentages based on number of organizations answering yes to question 13.)						
Access corporate accounting records (read only)	45	65	61	19	67	51
Data entry to corporate accounting records	36	46	44	31	33	32
Electronic mail	27	63	56	31	73	59
Sharing of peripheral equipment (such as printers and hard disks)	45	61	58	25	61	49
Access external data base (such as Dow Jones)	45	74	68	56	70	65
Other	0	26	21	13	9	10

17. In what area do you work? (*Note*: Percentages based on the total number of questionnaires returned.)

Finance/accounting	69	41	48	58	33	43
Data processing	25	39	36	28	38	33
Internal audit (EDP background)	6	12	10	2	13	8
Internal audit (accounting background)	19	20	19	8	12	11
Other	0	4	3	4	4	5

18. In what line of business does your company operate (predominantly)?

Manufacturing	50	37	40	40	45	42
Diversified	6	4	4	5	5	5
Finance	25	18	19	28	30	28
Retail	6	6	6	2	2	3
Education	6	6	6	2	8	5
Public Utility	0	2	1	0	2	1
Other	6	6	6	23	8	16

19. What is the total sales (or asset) volume (amount) of your company?

Less than $1,000,000	0	0	0	0	0	0
$1,000,000 to $4,999,999	6	0	1	5	0	3
$5,000,000 to $9,999,999	0	0	0	0	0	0
$10,000,000 to $49,999,999	13	4	6	8	7	7
$50,000,000 to $500,000,000	50	27	33	62	20	39
Over $500,000,000	31	69	60	25	73	51

	1986 Update			1984 Survey		
	Percentages for Companies Responding That Have:		Percentages for All Companies Responding to This Survey	Percentages for Companies Responding That Have:		Percentages for All Companies Responding to This Survey
Question	Less Than 25 Micro-computers	25 or More Micro-computers		Less Than 25 Micro-computers	25 or More Micro-computers	
20. How many microcomputers are installed at your company?						
0	0	0	0	0	0	0
1	6	0	1	5	0	2
2 to 4	31	0	7	32	0	16
5 to 24	63	0	15	63	0	30
25 to 49	0	16	12	0	20	10
50 to 100	0	25	19	0	23	11
More than 100	0	57	43	0	57	28
Do not know	0	2	1	0	0	3
21. How many microcomputers are installed in the finance/accounting areas?						
0	6	0	1	15	5	10
1	25	0	6	23	5	13
2 to 4	50	16	24	36	13	24
5 to 9	19	12	13	21	13	17
10 to 24	0	33	25	5	30	17
25 to 49	0	10	7	0	7	4
More than 50	0	22	16	0	22	11
Do not know	0	8	6	0	5	4

MICROCOMPUTER/DATA SECURITY SURVEY
1986 DATA SECURITY SUPPLEMENT

Question	Percentages for Companies Responding That Have:		Percentages for All Companies Responding to This Survey
	Less Than 25 Microcomputers	25 or More Microcomputers	
22. Has your company developed management policies that specifically address maintaining the integrity of programs and data files for microcomputers?			
Yes	25	27	27
No	75	73	73
If yes, have manuals, policy statements or other documentation containing those policies been distributed to microcomputer users? (*Note:* Percentages based on number of organizations answering yes to first part of this question.)			
Yes	100	64	72
No	0	36	28
And if yes, are microcomputer data security standards developed and monitored by those persons in your organization responsible for "traditional EDP environment" data security? (*Note:* Percentages based on number of organizations answering yes to first part of this question.)			
Yes	25	57	50
No	75	43	50
23. In general, does your company have written data security standards for files maintained on word processing equipment?			
Yes	6	22	18
No	94	78	82

Question	Percentages for Companies Responding That Have:		Percentages for All Companies Responding to This Survey
	Less Than 25 Micro-computers	25 or More Micro-computers	

24. In your company, are data security standards for microcomputers differentiated based on a risk analysis of particular installations' equipment configuration, communication capabilities and normal use?			
Yes	25	21	22
No	75	79	78
If yes, what department or group is responsible for the risk analysis and setting of installations' data security standards? (*Note:* Percentages based on number of all organizations answering yes to the first part of the question.)			
User	50	45	47
Data processing	50	45	47
Other	0	10	6

In general, what is the most important control objective of data security? Please rank the following in order of significance. (*Note:* Percentages based on number of all organizations responding to the question.)

	Rank 1	Rank 2	Rank 3
Preventing the theft of programs and data	16	31	53
Preventing the alteration or destruction of programs and data	55	27	18
Preventing the dissemination of confidential data within the company	38	37	25

25. Compared to the data security standards in effect for your company's larger computers, please rate your company's data security standards for microcomputers as much more restrictive (1), more restrictive (2), about the same (3), less restrictive (4), and much less restrictive (5), then indicate what relationship you believe is appropriate. (*Note:* The values are the averages of all respondents to the questionnaire.)

	Company Standards in Effect	Respondent Opinion
All micros—no difference by installation	3.6	3.0

Stand-alone micros only			3.5	3.1
Networked micros, "read only" capable			3.1	2.8
Networked micros, "read and write" capable			2.6	2.3

26. Is physical security and limited access to microcomputers more, less, or about the same in importance today for your company's data security standards compared to two years ago?

More important	43	45	44
Less important	7	4	5
About the same	50	51	51

27. For your company's stand-alone microcomputer installations, what data security standards are generally in effect? Please check those standards in effect at your company, and rate all (1—very important, 2—of moderate importance, and 3—not important).

Data security standards in effect (*Note*: Percentages based on total number of questionnaires returned.)

Restricted physical access	56	69	66
User passwords	50	57	55
Application passwords	38	37	37
Data encryption	19	20	19
Access logs	25	24	24
Time-out facility	13	24	21
Access attempt facility	13	24	21
Input/output (batch) controls	38	35	36
Program documentation	50	51	51
Control of changes in programs and data (version control)	38	45	43
Backup of program and data	88	76	79
Segregation of duties	38	39	39

Respondents' rating of data security standards (*Note*: Percentages based on all questionnaires returned.)

	Rank 1	Rank 2	Rank 3
Restricted physical access	34	49	17
User passwords	37	45	18
Application passwords	30	42	28
Data encryption	4	33	62

	Percentages for Companies Responding That Have:		Percentages for All Companies Responding to This Survey
Question	Less Than 25 Microcomputers	25 or More Microcomputers	
Access logs	6	40	54
Time-out facility	9	20	71
Access attempt facility	9	28	63
Input/output (batch) controls	32	32	36
Program documentation	58	30	11
Control of changes in programs and data (version control)	49	32	19
Backup of program and data	73	21	6
Segregation of duties	34	32	34

28. If your company's microcomputers are not currently networked with other computers, are there plans to establish a network within the next year?

Yes	13	18	16
No	62	33	41
Some/all micros already networked	25	49	43

If yes or already networked, what data security standards are planned for existing networks? Please rank in order of importance to your company.

Data security standards in effect (*Note*: Percentages based on number of organizations answering yes or already networked in the first part of the question.)

Read-but-not-write protection	17	50	45
Restricted physical access to micros	33	44	43
Multi-level user passwords	83	56	60
Terminal identification/application restriction codes	50	56	55
Automatic call-back checks	33	24	25
Access logs	67	32	38
Remote access blocked after hours	33	32	33

Time-out facility (disconnects terminals not communicating within specified time frame)	50	26	30
Access attempt facility (disconnects terminals after specified number of invalid access attempts)	33	38	38
Data entry range and reasonableness tests	67	35	40
Input (batch) controls where processing not on-line	67	32	38
Output controls	50	41	43
Data verification by operator	50	35	38
Control of changes in programs and data (version control)	33	44	43

29. Irrespective of your company's situation, where should the primary data access controls be implemented for microcomputers communicating with mainframes?

Microcomputer "read only" capable:			
At microcomputer to limit use or misuse of system applications and data	25	11	13
At mainframe since terminal application restriction codes, user passwords, and rules of use codes most probably in effect already	75	89	87
Microcomputer "read and write" capable:			
At microcomputer to limit use or misuse of system applications and data	18	17	18
At mainframe since terminal application restriction codes, user passwords, and rules of use codes most probably in effect already	82	83	82

30. Has access to mainframe programs and data become more or less restricted in your company since the original survey?

More restricted	36	40	39
Less restricted	18	10	12
About the same	45	50	49

31. If access is now more restricted, what were the reasons for the change? (*Note*: Percentages based on number of reasons checked in the aggregate.)

Increased number of micro-to-mainframe communication links	29	20	21
Implementation of "on-line" data entry applications	29	18	19

Question	Percentages for Companies Responding That Have:		Percentages for All Companies Responding to This Survey
	Less Than 25 Micro-computers	25 or More Micro-computers	
Installation of hardware/software to facilitate remote "dial-up" communications	0	25	21
Increase in data files maintained in mainframes linked to local area networks	14	8	9
Adverse publicity about computer fraud or loss of data or programs due to deliberate intervention by computer "hackers" (not necessarily affecting your company)	29	13	15
Other	0	18	15
32. If your company has networks with electronic or voice mail, have controls been implemented to prevent network users from "browsing" through other users' message files?			
Yes	19	47	40
No	81	53	60
If yes, has utilization of electronic mail increased or decreased since controls were enhanced? (*Note:* Percentages based on number of organizations answering yes in the first part of the question.)			
Increased	67	38	41
Decreased	0	0	0
About the same	33	63	59
33. Overall, do you feel your company's data security standards for microcomputers are too stringent, reasonable or not strong enough?			
Too stringent	0	0	0
Not strong enough	54	68	65
Reasonable	46	32	35

GLOSSARY

This glossary is presented as an aid to understanding some of the technical jargon associated with computers.

Access time. The time it takes for data to be located on a secondary-storage medium, read from that medium, and transferred to the CPU.

Acoustic coupler. Electromechanical equipment that has two rubber cups at each end for receiving the mouthpiece and earpiece of a telephone receiver. You use an acoustic coupler, which is a type of modem, to send information via a standard telephone. The acoustic coupler translates computer signals into audio signals, which a telephone can then transmit to a computer at the other end.

Alphanumeric. Literally, letters (alpha) and numbers (numeric). The term is used to describe letters, noncomputational numbers (e.g., as used in a title), punctuation marks, and graphics characters.

Analog computer. A computer that processes continuous-wave data (such as temperature or weight) by measuring this data to within a certain precision.

Application software. A set of programs that performs specific tasks for users.

Artificial intelligence (AI). A branch of computer science that is involved with using computer programs to solve problems that appear to require human deductive reasoning.

ASCII. An acronym for American National Standard Code for Information Interchange. A standard code used to exchange information among data-processing and communications systems.

Assembler. A type of language translator that converts programs, commands, and statements from assembly language to machine language.

Assembly language. A computer language by which a programmer can enter commands resembling machine-language commands in their function, but which are easier to use because they are in symbolic form.

Asynchronous transmission. A method of transmitting data that permits the time interval between transmitted characters to be of unequal length.

Autodial. A function that enables a modem to dial telephone numbers.

Backup. A copy of any program or data stored typically in machine-readable form (e.g., disk, magnetic tape). Backups should be stored in a safe place and used if a problem develops with the original. Frequently used and important information and programs should always have backups.

BASIC. A popular computer language invented for educational purposes. An acronym for Beginner's All-Purpose Symbolic Instruction Code. This language is used for programming many small systems.

Batch processing. A technique in which a number of similar items or transactions to be processed are grouped (batched) and processed in a designated sequence during a computer run. Often referred to as sequential processing.

Baud. A measure of data-transmission speed that is roughly equivalent to bits per second (bps). For example, a 1200-baud modem transmits data at approximately 1200 bps.

Binary code. A language that makes use of two characters, usually 0 and 1. A machine language.

Bit. Contraction of binary digit. An electronic signal or a piece of data, or a number, that is viewed as having one of two states: on or off, one or zero, yes or no. Bits are used in electronic systems to encode orders (instructions) and data. Bits are usually grouped in nybbles (four), bytes (eight or nine), or larger units.

Block. A collection of contiguous records that can be read from an input device or written to an output device with a single computer command.

Boot. The action of starting or "bringing in" the operating-system program and making the system and the computer available to the user. Generally, this happens automatically when the system is turned on. If a difficulty arises, the system may be rebooted by pressing the reset button on the computer.

Bootstrap. A program used to start (or "boot") the computer, usually by clearing the memory, setting up various devices, and loading the operating system from input/output internal or external memory.

BPI. Bits per inch. A measure of data density on, for example, magnetic tape.

BPS. Bits per second. A measure of the speed of data transmission.

Break. Applies to a key on most keyboards that is used to tell the computer that the current operation is to be aborted.

Broadband. A classification of a communications channel describing the fastest speed of data transport. Generally considered to be anything exceeding 1200 characters per second.

Buffer area. A temporary-storage area within main memory that compensates for the differences in rates of flow of data from peripheral devices and within the CPU.

Bug. A problem with a program or a mistake in software.

Bus. A circuit or group of circuits that provides an electronic pathway between two or more microprocessors or input/output devices, such as a keyboard and a computer. A bus is also a type of network topology.

Byte. A collection of eight (sometimes nine) bits or electronic signals that, when taken together, represent a piece of information or a machine-language program instruction.

Called subroutines. A series of instructions designed to perform a limited task, such as a net present-value calculation or a fluctuation analysis.

Cathode-ray tube (CRT). A display screen for presenting information and graphics.

Central-processing unit (CPU). The portion of the computer that interprets programs and does arithmetic and logical operations to solve problems. The CPU in a microcomputer is contained on a single microprocessor chip.

Character printer. A printer that prints only a character at a time.

Chip. A number of electronic circuits that perform a few to a large number of functions. These electronic circuits can be manufactured and put into a chip of silicon about one-quarter-inch square or smaller. The chip is mounted onto a socket that has a number of projecting pins. These pins fit into a receptacle on a printed circuit board.

Circuit board. See Printed circuit board.

COBOL. An acronym for Common Business-Oriented Language. A high-level language developed for business data-processing applications.

Communications controller. A device that directs flow of information in computer networks. This device is normally used when a mainframe computer is part of the network.

Compiler. A type of language translator that converts programs, commands, and statements from a third- or fourth-generation language into machine language.

Compressed printing. By reducing the distance between verticals in a dot-matrix printer, characters can be made to print narrower, although of the same height, so that there are more characters per inch and thus a compressed format.

Console. A device that provides a keyboard and a display, usually for direct entry into a microcomputer system.

Control section. The part of the CPU that selects, interprets, and oversees the execution of program instructions.

CP/M. Control Program for Microcomputers, a widely used operating system developed and sold by Digital Research, Inc.

CPU. See Central-processing unit.

Cursor. A marker (dot of light) that appears on the video screen to indicate the next entry position. The marker might be an underline that is stable or blinks, or a rectangle that contains a marker in reverse video, either static or blinking.

Cursor key. A key that, when pressed, causes the cursor to move in a designated direction. Arrows engraved on the keys indicate direction of cursor movement: up, down, right, left, or home (top left corner of screen).

Cycle time. The time it takes a computer to obtain and interpret an instruction from memory, retrieve data from memory, process the data, return the data to memory, and determine the location of the next instruction. A measure of the speed of a computer.

Daisy wheel. A print element for several popular printers consisting of a plastic or metal disk with spokes radiating from the center portion. At the end of each spoke is a circular area with a typeface impression on it. This little disk is like the petals of a flower, hence the name "daisy wheel."

Database. A stored collection of data that is needed by organizations and individuals to meet their information-processing and retrieval requirements. Any group of related records.

Database administrator. The person responsible for defining, updating, and controlling design, maintenance, and access to a computer database.

Database-management system (DBMS). The comprehensive software system that builds, maintains, and provides access to a database.

Data communications. The transfer of data between CPUs and external devices or terminals. Also known as teleprocessing.

Data dictionary/directory system. A repository of definitions of data contained in a database. Typically includes the name, type, usage, field size, and source of the data, and the application programs authorized to access the data. Collectively referred to as a data dictionary.

Debug. To correct mistakes in a program or software.

Density. The closeness with which information is packed on a medium. It is measured linearly in terms of bits per inch. It is measured radially on the disk in terms of tracks per inch.

Digital computer. Counting device designed for processing pulse-code data that comes in the form of discrete, separable units. Virtually all computers used for financial applications are digital computers.

Direct access. A method of data access in which any individual data element can be accessed without accessing any others beforehand. Also called random access. See Sequential access.

Direct-access storage device (DASD). A secondary-storage device, such as a magnetic disk (drive), that allows data to be accessed directly.

Direct-connect modem. A modem that plugs directly into a telephone outlet, bypassing the handset.

Disk. A flat, circular object that resembles a phonograph record. As a record "stores" music, a disk stores information. The disk is inserted into a disk drive that rotates at high speed. The drive writes new information onto the disk and reads information that is already stored on the disk. There are two major types of disks used with microcomputers: flexible floppy disks (diskettes) and hard disks (often called "Winchester" disks).

Disk controller. Circuitry for controlling one or more disk drives. Usually the controller circuitry is on its own printed circuit board, which plugs into a bus: it can control eight or more disk drives, although few systems use more than four drives and two is the usual number. Control signals from the CPU select and direct one of the disk drives. Status signals from the controller tell the CPU the progress of the activity. Data is reorganized by the controller as it passes between the drive and memory.

Disk drive. A device that reads, at a very high speed, computerized data stored on magnetic media called disks. The disks can be flexible or floppy (made of soft, pliable plastic and metallic oxide) or can be stiff or hard (made of rigid plastic and metallic oxide).

Diskette. A single removable plastic disk in its own paper envelope. Due to its flexibility, it is called a "floppy" disk.

Distributed data-processing (DDP) system. A data-processing system comprising a coordinated set of information-processing capabilities implemented in two or more relatively independent resource centers linked together by data-communications facilities.

Documentation. Generally, the written set of instructions that tells how to use software or hardware. It also refers to all the information that a person gathers while writing a program so others can determine how the program was written and, therefore, be able to modify it or correct problems.

Dot-matrix printer. A printer, either impact or nonimpact, that prints a pattern of small dots to form a character.

Double-density diskette. A diskette manufactured with a new technology that can hold twice as much data as diskettes manufactured at the standard density.

Double-sided diskette. A double-sided diskette provides two surfaces on which data may be written by the computer. This doubles the amount of storage that each diskette provides. It requires that the drive have two read/write heads selectable by the computer.

Download. The ability to transfer data from a larger (host) computer to a smaller computer.

EBCDIC. A acronym for Extended Binary Coded Decimal Interchange Code. A standard 8-bit code used to represent data in certain computers.

Editor. A program by which text can be entered into the computer memory, displayed on the screen, and manipulated by the user. An aid for writing a program. The central component of a word processor.

Emulation. Simulation of a system, function, or program.

Encryption. A technique for guarding against unauthorized reading/ modifying data being transmitted. Uses software or a special hardware device prior to transmission that converts data to a code masking the meaning of the data until it is decoded at the destination.

Erasable programmable read-only memory (EPROM). A form of ROM that can be programmed, erased, and reprogrammed. Usually found in the form of a chip.

Expanded printing. Type of printing whereby the user increases the spacing between verticals for a dot-matrix printer to print characters that are wider but of the same height so there are fewer characters per inch.

External memory. Memory used to store programs and information that would be lost if the computer were turned off. Cassette tapes, disks, and Winchester disks are examples. External memory is also known as mass memory and removable memory.

Field. A group of related characters treated as a unit (e.g., a group of adjacent numbers used to represent an hourly wage rate). An item in a record.

File. A logical collection of data designated by name and considered as a unit by a user. A file is physically divided into smaller records.

File area. The area on the disk available for storage of files containing data or programs.

File directory. The disk area allocated to hold a table of contents that names and indicates the area occupied by each file as well as the available space on the disk.

Formatting. The action of checking and writing whatever information is needed by the system on a previously unused disk. For a hard disk, this usually means writing all data tracks with track identifiers and filling data fields with a fixed character to show that the tract is empty. Soft sectoring requires writing tract and sector identification at the beginning of each sector of every tract. Some formatting programs attempt to verify the ability to write and read successfully on every sector.

FORTRAN. An acronym for FORmula TRANslator. A high-level language used primarily for scientific, mathematical, and engineering programs.

Fourth-generation language. A human-language-like, user-friendly, nonprocedural language used to program and/or read and reorganize data.

Front-end processor. A programmable communications processor.

Full duplex. A method of communication between computers that permits simultaneous transmission in both directions.

Gateway. Hardware and software used to connect two computer systems or networks. For example, a gateway is used to connect a LAN to another LAN.

Half duplex. A method of communication between computers that permits transmission in either direction but not both simultaneously.

Handshaking. The exchange of predetermined signals between two computers or between a computer and peripheral equipment, such as a modem or printer. Handshaking allows the computer to ascertain whether another device is present and ready to transmit or receive data.

Hard disk. A data-storage medium with a storage capacity 10 to 30 or more times that of a floppy disk.

Hardware. Physical equipment; electronic, magnetic, and mechanical devices (e.g., printers, tape drives, and CPUs).

High-level language. A programming language oriented toward the problem to be solved or the procedures to be used. Instructions are given to a computer by using convenient letters, symbols, or human language-like text. A high-level language is passed through a compiler or an interpreter to produce the 1s and 0s that the computer understands.

Host. A larger computer, typically a mainframe or minicomputer, that maintains corporate data and is connected to a network of smaller computers or terminals.

Immediate-update processing. The timing of data processing in which data is processed as transactions are initially entered.

Information center. An alternative to developing new computerized information systems in which authorized users have easy access to the organization's databases.

Input/Output (I/O). The process of a computer accepting data from or writing data to a device, such as a disk drive.

Interactive data entry. The mode of data entry in which data can be corrected at the time of entry.

Interactive system. One that permits direct communication and dialog between users and the application programs operating in the computer.

Interface. Any hardware or software system that links a computer with any other device.

Interpreter. A program that translates from third- or fourth-generation language to machine language a statement at a time as the data is processed.

Kilobyte (K). 1024 (2 to the 10th power) bytes of data.

LAN. See Local-area network.

Language. In relation to computers, any unified, related set of commands or instructions that the computer can accept. Low-level languages are difficult to use but closely resemble the fundamental operations of the computer. High-level languages resemble human language.

Language, assembly. A low-level language by which a programmer can enter commands that resemble machine-language commands in their function, but which are easier to use because they are in symbolic form.

Language, machine. The binary ones and zeros found in memory that constitute a command as interpreted by the computer hardware.

Language, procedure-oriented. A language for programming whereby procedures for performing logical actions are easily written. Sometimes called a "compiler language." Examples of such languages are BASIC, COBOL, and FORTRAN.

Laser printer. A very fast line printer that uses a laser beam to form character images on the surface of a rotating drum. A toner that adheres to the images is then transferred to the paper.

Leased line. A telephone line reserved for private use by a single customer.

Light pen. An input device that allows a terminal user to choose among alternatives. When a menu is presented on the screen, for instance, a number of choices are given the operator, each with a box next to it. The operator positions the light pen to a box representing his or her choice and then presses the entry button on the pen. The pen contains a light sensor that returns a signal, which indicates to the computer which choice the operator has made.

Line feed. The action of advancing the paper or the cursor so that it is aligned to feed the next line below the previous one.

Line multiplexor. A data-communications device that transforms relatively low-speed data from a number of terminals to a high-speed single stream of data for transmission on a single communications channel.

Line printer. A printer that has a print mechanism that is rotating constantly at a high speed. The mechanism might be a drum, a chain, a train, a band, or a belt. Printing occurs whenever a print slug arrives at the position at which it should be printed and then a hammer strikes it to make an impression on the paper. Hence, different character positions of the line are printed almost randomly. Only when all the characters for the line have been printed does the paper advance. Prints an entire line at a time.

Local-area network (LAN). A data-communications network used by an organization to link together nearby devices, such as computers, terminals, and word-processing stations.

Machine language. The language (1s or 0s) used directly by the computer.

Magnetic-ink character reader (MICR). A data-input device that reads magnetic characters, such as those printed at the bottom of checks.

Mainframe. A powerful high-speed computer usually designed for near-simultaneous processing of many programs.

Main memory. The storage section of the central-processing unit that holds instructions and data. Also called primary storage, real memory, or memory.

Master file. A file containing relatively permanent data. This file is updated by records in a transaction file.

Matrix printer. An impact-printing mechanism containing a number of small, thin, flexible rods that make an impression on the paper as a series of vertical columns of dots. A character is formed by combining a number of these vertical columns.

Megabyte. 1,048,576 (2 to the 20th power) bytes of data.

Memory. See Main memory.

Memory, random-access (RAM). A memory that can be altered by the computer in a fraction of a microsecond.

Memory, read-only (ROM). A memory from which the computer can read information at will but cannot alter or change the information stored there.

Memory, programmable, read-only (PROM). A read-only memory into which data can be written by an external programming device.

Microcomputer. A small but complete computer system, including CPU, memory, input/output (I/O) interfaces, and power supply. The smallest category of computer, consisting of a microprocessor and associated storage and input/output elements.

Microcomputer chip. The microprocessor chip contains the circuitry of the CPU. It is mounted in one socket of the CPU board.

Microprocessor board (CPU board). A printed circuit board for which the main component is the microprocessor chip. It contains other components, such as those to generate the timing signals and to shape the pulses necessary to run the microprocessor.

Mnemonic. A set of letters that represents the activity performed by a command. It suggests these actions so that the programmer can more easily recall the meaning of the alphanumeric character that represents the command (e.g., LDA = Load the A register).

Modem. Modulator-demodulator. A device that transforms a computer's electrical pulses into audible tones for transmission over a telephone line to another computer. A modem also receives incoming tones and transforms them into electrical signals that can be processed and stored by the computer.

Monitor. A display unit (like a TV screen) containing a CRT, video amplifiers, horizontal and vertical scanning and synchronization circuits, and power supply.

Motherboard. A printed circuit board onto which other printed circuit boards connect.

Multiprocessing. The connecting of multiple CPUs within a computerized information system to allow for simultaneous processing of more than one program.

Multiprogramming. The processing of multiple jobs in an integrated fashion so that the CPU is operating almost constantly rather than waiting for slower input/output devices. Also known as multitasking.

Multitasking. See Multiprogramming.

Narrowband. A classification of a communications channel describing the slowest speed of data transport, generally considered to be less than 30 characters per second. Also known as baseband.

Network. An interconnected group of computers (including microcomputers) or terminals linked together by a transmission facility. An interconnection of computer systems and/or peripheral devices at dispersed locations that exchange data as necessary to perform the various functions.

Node. A computer or terminal location in a communications network.

Nonprocedural language. A computerized language allowing the user to describe to the computer what information is desired and in what format, rather than describing the procedures to be followed in obtaining the information.

Object program. A set of computer instructions that has been translated by an assembler, compiler, or interpreter into machine language.

On-line. A term describing persons, equipment, or devices that are in direct communication with the computer.

On-line editor. Systems software designed to enable programmers to enter and modify source code as well as execute processing jobs in an on-line environment.

Operating system. A collection of programs that control a computer's internal functions.

Optical-character reader. A data-input device that reads alphanumeric characters and bar codes.

Optical disks. A data-storage medium that employs laser technology to burn tiny pits onto a disk. This is a relatively new technology for mass-storage of data.

Packaged software. A program designed for a specific application of broad, general usage, unadapted to any particular installation.

Packet. A group of data that is transmitted in a specified format.

Packet network. An electronic message-carrying system that allows computers and terminals in different locations one-way and two-way communication with each other. Packet networks (sometimes called "value-added networks") allow different kinds of computers to communicate with one another.

Parity bit. An extra bit added to a character's binary code, which can be used to detect transmission errors.

Password. A predetermined code word that should be known only to the person(s) intended to use it. Used to control access to protected elements of a computerized information system, such as data files, terminals, libraries, or application-program functions.

PBX. An acronym for Private Branch Exchange. A telephone communications system serving a specific location, such as an office or building.

Peripheral device. Device that performs input, output or both, such as a printer, terminal, keyboard, or disk drive.

Plotter. An output device driven by the computer, which moves a pen across a sheet of paper, lifting it away from the paper in some areas and putting it down in others to create a multiple-line pattern.

Polling. A method of controlling transmission of data by asking each particular computer or terminal (in sequence) in a network if it wishes to transmit data.

Printed circuit board. A laminated plastic board, about a sixteenth of an inch thick, onto which wiring is electroplated. This wiring connects components and sockets, which are fastened to the board. The sockets receive chips. A printed circuit board constitutes a complete functional unit, such as a memory or a processor. One of the edges of the board is set up so that all the wires that leave or enter the board appear there as thin printed lines. This edge fits into a receptacle that connects it to other components of the computer. There are many types of circuit boards, including memory boards, processor boards, and so forth.

Printer, bidirectional. The ability of a printer to print on paper when the carriage is moving either to the right or to the left. This speeds up printing because it eliminates carriage returns during which no printing can take place.

Printer, impact. A printer in which the character is formed on the paper by the impact of a hammer hitting a typed slug against an inked ribbon to impart an inked impression on the paper.

Printer, ink-jet. A nonimpact printer that uses multiple jets of ink turned on or off to form a character as a matrix of dots.

Printer, nonimpact. A printer that does not use impact to form a character on paper but rather uses heat, light, electric current, or a jet of ink.

Program, application. A program written to solve a user's problem.

Program, utility. Programs written by a supplier to provide standard services for the user. They do not usually perform an application function.

Prompt. A symbol presented on the CRT screen to tell the user that the system is ready to accept a new command or line of text.

Protocol. A set of codes that must be transmitted and received in the proper sequence to guarantee that the desired terminals are hooked together and can "talk" as desired.

Query language. A fourth-generation language enabling the user to read and reorganize data, but not to alter data. Query languages are most often used in a database environment.

RAM. An acronym for random-access memory; internal memory generally used to store data and application programs.

Read/write head. The part of a disk or tape reader that either picks up the electromagnetic signals from the disk or tape for transferring to the CPU or writes the data (electromagnetic signals) on the disk or tape.

Real time. Descriptive of on-line computer processing systems that receive and process data quickly enough to produce output to control, direct or affect the outcome of an ongoing activity, or process.

Record. A collection of related items of data treated as a unit.

Register. A small and fast-operating hardware device for temporarily holding data. The computer, memory, and external devices all use registers to hold both data and status information.

Remote terminal. A terminal (display and keyboard) that does not necessarily have computing power near at hand and communicates with the computing power by means of communication lines, such as telephone lines.

Report generator. A type of computer program that enables one to retrieve from stored data analyses of, for example, customers or inventory items.

ROM. Read-only memory, semi-conductor chips containing preprogrammed instructions that cannot be changed by the user.

RS-232-C. An electrical standard used for data communication.

Secondary storage. Storage outside the central-processing unit that holds data and instructions. Examples are magnetic disk and tape.

Sector. A portion of a track lying between two sector holes or as defined by the formatting process.

Sector hole. A hole in a hard-sectored disk. There are a fixed number of such holes around the circumference of a circle of fixed radius. There is a single hole in the envelope. Each time a sector hole passes underneath this hole in the envelope, a sector pulse is optically generated.

Security software. Systems software designed to limit access to sensitive resources, such as data files, program libraries, and terminals.

Sequential access. A requirement of the file that accessing a record requires scanning through all the intermediate records from the starting position. Sequential access is an inherent feature of a medium that must be reviewed in a fixed order, such as magnetic tape.

Single-density disk. Diskettes, as originally developed, that could read and write at approximately 3200 bits per inch, a density known as single density.

Software. The set of programs that instruct the computer to tell it how to access, process, and store data.

Source program. A set of computer instructions written by a programmer in a programming language (e.g., COBOL, FORTRAN). The source program must be converted into machine language to be understood by the computer.

Synchronous transmission. A method of transmitting data that requires a definite time interval between transmitted characters.

Systems software. The set of programs that allows the application software to process data using a computer.

Telecommunications. Any communication between computers, or devices with embedded computers, in various locations. This communication usually takes place over long distances and usually is carried out over phone lines, radio waves, or a satellite-transmission apparatus.

Teleprocessing monitor. Systems software designed to control the execution of application programs in an on-line environment.

Terminal. A device with a keyboard for input and a printer or video screen (CRT) for output through which data is sent to and received from a computer.

Terminal, dumb. A visual-display terminal incapable of processing data but capable of sending to or receiving from a central computer.

Terminal, intelligent. A visual-display terminal with a microprocessor built in for complete editing facilities and processing capability.

Terminal, smart. A terminal with built-in programmable editing facilities that allows a full screen of data to be collected and sent to the computer or to be collected for display from the computer.

Timesharing. The near-simultaneous use of hardware by a number of devices and programs in such a way as to provide quick response to each of the users.

Topology. Physical configuration of a network. Common topologies are the star, ring, and bus.

Track. The circular area swept out by the head when it occupies one of the fixed standard positions. Tracks are numbered from outside in, starting from zero and going to the maximum for a particular disk.

Transfer rate. For a disk or other peripheral device, the rate at which information is moved from the device to memory, or vice versa. The customary unit is kilobits per second (kbs). This should not be confused with kilobytes per second. A transfer rate for single-density diskettes is 250 kilobits per second and that for double density is 500 kilobits per second.

Transmission medium. The wire, cable, and so forth used to connect nodes in a network. The most common types are twisted-pair wires, coaxial cable, and fiber-optic cable.

TTY. An abbreviation for teletype equipment.

Turnkey system. A complete system in which all equipment and software is installed and debugged by one vendor.

Upload. The ability to transfer data from a smaller computer to a larger (host) computer.

Utility program. Systems software designed to perform useful administrative functions, such as sorting records into a particular sequence, merging and copying files, and printing file dumps. Utilities usually do not perform application functions.

Value-added network. A data-communications network operated by an organization that generally leases the communications media of a common carrier, then adds a value by making the communication more efficient to its customers.

Virtual storage. The capability to use on-line secondary-storage devices, disks, and specialized software to divide programs into smaller segments for transmission to and from internal storage to significantly increase the effective size of internal storage.

Visual-display terminal. A device with a keyboard for input and a printer or video screen (CRT) for output through which data is sent to and received from a computer.

Voiceband. A classification of a communications channel describing the middle range of speed of data transport. Generally considered to be 50–1200 characters per second.

Volatile. A memory in which information storage continues as long as the power is maintained. When the power is turned off, the information in memory is lost.

Winchester disk. A form of hard-disk technology. See Disk and Hard disk.

Window. A portion of a display characterized differently from the rest of the screen. A window may show letters of magnified size or from a different area of memory.

Word. A group of bits or characters treated as an entity and capable of being stored together at one location.

Write protect. Each diskette (or other storage medium) has a notch (or logically similar approach) in one corner that is optically scanned to inhibit writing on those disks for which protection is desired. Generally, this notch must be covered to protect the disk; if the notch is not covered, the disk is not protected.

INDEX

Acceptance, procedures, 16, 89–90
Access, controls, 20–21, 23, 27, 38, 114–115, 121, 123
Applications, generation, 91
Architecture, system, 87
Auditing, EDP, 41–43, 52–53
Audit trails, 94
Automated teller machines (ATM), 105

Central processing unit (CPU), 100–102, 128
Changes, program, 13, 24, 75–77, 94–97
Charges, for data processing, 13
Circuits, transmission, 127
Common (centrally-developed) systems, 64
Communications, *see* Telecommunications
Computer-assisted-audit-testing (CAAT), 42
Concentrator, 124–125
Consultants, outside, 79–81
Continuity, of processing, 5, 20, 25–26, 27, 34–35, 46
Costs/cost-benefits, 5, 13–14, 44

Databases administrations and management systems, 23, 60–63, 66, 73–74, 111–116
Data dictionary, 113, 114
Data processing, management and organization, 3, 11, 12, 16, 27, 39, 46, 63
Data security, 11, 19, 30, 34, 51–56, 62, 74
  group, 78–79, 81
  review, 45–46, 79–80

Development of systems, 83–97
Disaster recovery, *see* Continuity, of processing
Distributed processing, 63–66, 123
Documentation, 16, 23, 26, 30, 34, 89–90, 92–94, 96

EDP department, *see* Data processing, management and organization
Encryption, 129, 131

Feasibility studies, 85
File access manager systems, 111
File conversion, 87
Fraud, 30–31, 70, 123

Hackers, computer, 21, 45
Hardware, 99–106

Identification codes, *see* Passwords
Implementation planning, 87
Information centers, 72–73
Input/Output controls, 35–36
Integrated test facilities, 45
Integrity of data, 5, 23, 36, 39, 80
Internal auditors, 5, 15, 17, 41–50, 79, 84–85, 90, 96
Interruption of operations, *see* Continuity, of processing

Librarian software/libraries, 16, 75, 78, 96, 117, 121

181

INDEX

Local area networks (LANS), 130, 133–138
Logs, activity, 22, 24, 74, 94, 128

Magnetic tape, 103
Mainframes, 99
Maintenance, 11, 21, 75, 83, 95–97
Management trail, 94
Message authentication, 129
Microcomputer-mainframe links, 37–38
Microcomputers, 29–40, 52, 54, 64, 66, 99, 133–138
Microfilm (COM), 105
Minicomputers, 99
Misconceptions computer-related, 5–7
Modem, 125
Modifications to systems or programs, *see* Changes, program
Multiplexors, 124–125
Multiprocessing, 109
Myths, computer-related, 5–7

Networks, 65, 129–138

Operating systems, 108–110
Optical character readers (OCR), 105
Optical disks, 103
Organization charts and structure, 11–12, 16, 42, 68–73

Passwords, 21, 22, 52, 54–55, 70
Planning of systems, 9–17, 68, 80
Point-of-sale terminals, 105
Policy maker and action, 3–5, 8, 39–40, 41, 43, 52, 66
Post-implementation review, 90
Printers, 105
Private networks, 130–131
Processing controls, 24
Program, generation, 90
Project teams, 15–16

Prototyping, 90–91
Public switched networks, 131–132

Quality control, 15, 17

Random access memory (RAM), 100–101
Read-only memory (ROM), 101
Requirements, definition, 86, 91

Sabotage, 30, 70
Security, *see* Data security
Security software, 54, 73, 77, 116–117
Segregation-of-duties, 11, 23
Software, 107–121
Storage, secondary, 102–103
System, design and development, 11, 48, 73–75, 83–95
System management methodology (SMM), 84–93

Tape, *see* Magnetic tape, 103
Technology, monitoring/emerging, 7–10, 49, 59–66
Telecommunications, 21, 45, 60, 65, 118–120, 123, 138
Terminals, 104–105, 127
Testing, 24, 88–89, 96
Translators, computer language, 110–111

Unit testing, 88–89
Users/user groups, 13, 15–16, 23, 29, 63, 83–84, 108
Utility programs, 118

Value added networks, 132–133
Virtual storage, 109
Voice response systems, 105

Wide-area networks, 103–133